101 Business Ideas That Will Change the Way You Work

Praise ... he Way
by Antonio E. Weiss

'Weiss has done an invaluable service to managers by c   g an enticing sample dish of the biggest ideas in business and social science. His book offers a short, sharp education in the essentials.'
Philip Delves Broughton, author of the New York Times bestseller What They Teach You at Harvard Business School

'What fun. A box of chocolates for the managerial mind, containing many surprises, some chestnuts given new meaning, and a year's worth of intellectual nutrition.'
Walter Kiechel III, author of The Lords of Strategy

'I greatly admire Antonio's work and writing and Pearson's record in bringing the best thoughts and practice in business to a global market.'
Sir Alcon Copisarow, first non-American senior partner at McKinsey & Company and chairman of trustees of the Eden Project

'The gap between business academics and business people is bad for both. This book makes a valuable and stimulating contribution to bridging the gap.'
David R. Kaye, former partner with Andersen Consulting and former dean of the City University Business School (now Cass Business School)

'Here is your chance to use the latest findings in your organisation. These business ideas will help you rethink your strategy and your approach as a manager. Bringing the best academic insights to the real problems we all face is truly clever thinking!'
Christopher McKenna, Saïd Business School, University of Oxford and author of The World's Newest Profession

'Antonio Weiss has synthesised key concepts from business research and practice in a manner that is both erudite and highly readable. This book will challenge the way you think about business and help you see the world and the people around you more clearly. It is a book to be read once and then dipped into many times.'
Morgen Witzel, fellow, Centre for Leadership Studies, University of Exeter Business School and author of A History of Management Thought

101 Business Ideas That Will Change the Way You Work

Turning Clever Thinking Into Smart Advice

Antonio E. Weiss

PEARSON

Harlow, England • London • New York • Boston • San Francisco • Toronto • Sydney
Auckland • Singapore • Hong Kong • Tokyo • Seoul • Taipei • New Delhi
Cape Town • São Paulo • Mexico City • Madrid • Amsterdam • Munich • Paris • Milan

Pearson Education Limited
Edinburgh Gate
Harlow CM20 2JE
United Kingdom
Tel: +44 (0)1279 623623
Web: www.pearson.com/uk

First published 2013

Pearson Education is not responsible for the content of third-party Internet sites.

ISBN: 978-0-273-78619-1 (print)
          978-0-273-79455-4 (PDF)
          978-0-273-79456-1 (ePub)

British Library Cataloguing-in-Publication Data
A catalogue record for the print edition is available from the British Library

Library of Congress Cataloguing-in-Publication Data
A catalogue record for the print edition is available from the Library of Congress

10 9 8 7 6 5 4 3 2 1
17 16 15 14 13

Illustrations: Mercedes León
Cover design: Dan Mogford

Print edition typeset in 9.5pt Scene Regular by 3
Print by Ashford Colour Press Ltd., Gosport

NOTE THAT ANY PAGE CROSS-REFERENCES REFER TO THE PRINT EDITION

Contents

PART 2
IDEAS ABOUT PERFORMANCE

PART 3
IDEAS ABOUT ORGANISATIONS 251

About the author

Antonio E. Weiss is a writer and management consultant. His previous book, *Key Business Solutions* (Financial Times Prentice Hall, 2011), was shortlisted for the Chartered Management Institute Management Book of the Year Award 2013, featured as a WHSmith Business Bestseller, and has been translated into several languages across the globe. He also writes regularly for publications such as *The Guardian* and *Prospect*, presents at conferences on economic, business and political issues, and has been featured on international media including ABC Radio Australia and BBC Radio 4. As a consultant, he has advised leading public- and private-sector bodies on major strategy, capability building and performance improvement issues. Antonio is also a board member of one of the largest further education colleges in London. He holds a bachelor's degree (first class) and master's degree (distinction) in history from the University of Cambridge. Antonio is contactable via his website (www.antonioweiss.com).

Acknowledgements

This book owes a huge debt of gratitude to the researchers and writers whose fascinating studies are contained within its pages. Thanks to their work every day startling discoveries are made that help improve our understanding of how – and why – we work as we do, and how we can improve. This book can only hope to cast a light on the tremendous research undertaken, and I strongly urge readers to dive into the further references to find many more treasures.

On a more personal note, I am always grateful to my friends and colleagues at 2020 Delivery – the UK's leading public service specialist management consultancy – for the support they have continued to give me throughout my career. Working there is a genuine pleasure. I am also particularly grateful for the continued backing of everyone at Pearson, and especially my editor, Nicole Eggleton who has been a delight to work with. Readers will also undoubtedly have enjoyed the wonderful illustrations of Mercedes León – I am thrilled to have had someone so brilliant work on this book with me.

Finally, I thank my family for their love and support and, in particular, my wife, Carol. Much of this book was written in the run-up to our wedding, and I'm aware that from an organisation and timing point of view this was not ideal! This book is dedicated, with much love, to her.

INTRODUCTION AND IDEA #1:
How to turn theory into results

Bridge the link between business and world-class research and you will reap huge benefits.

What you need to know

What makes a great CEO? How can I improve my chances of getting a promotion? Should we trust these experts' predictions? For too long, business questions like these have been answered with the retort 'we don't know and we can't know – just trust your judgement.' Well, what if we actually now know a lot more than most people think, and most of the time our judgement is hopelessly wrong? In fact, this is the reality of the situation. For several decades, academics and researchers have been investigating some of the critical questions that businesspeople are desperate for answers to, and they have come up with some fascinating replies. To date, however, far too little attention has been devoted to their amazing discoveries. This book aims to bring their groundbreaking findings to you.

Why you need to read this book

How often do you read advice that 'the best way to run this team is to give them autonomy'? Or that customers 'like to be listened to'? Or even that great leaders 'are born, not made'? Well, where does this advice come from? Who says it works? Does it even work? If you've ever found the amount of evidence in management and leadership advice lacking, this book is for you. Mining the latest in world-class research from all fields of academia, *101 Business Ideas* has focused on some of the major topics in business and carefully synthesised what the key research on each has concluded. At the end, you'll know: the secret to how long recruiters actually spend reading résumés; how swearing is a powerful painkiller; how to tell if a business leader is lying; how Superman can improve your confidence; why all your products should be like IKEA's; and much, much more. Read on!

A word of warning

Just as every strong argument has a counter-argument, every great idea and piece of research will inevitably provoke debate or analysis that questions it. At all times, this book has sought to provide the most balanced approach possible when summarising the available research. However, inevitably, some topics will evoke more debate than others. There will always be caveats to research findings. For example, if a study in Japan shows that consumers prefer bundled packaged goods over discounts, does this mean consumers in America also share this preference? Such an inference would require several assumptions to be accepted. As a consequence, while each *Idea* covered in this book is accompanied by some tips as to how you can change your working styles, on occasions it has been necessary to push some research conclusions to their logical, practical end. Whether this is advisable has always been a source of passionate debate for academics. As such, at the end of every chapter, references have been provided for the key texts for each topic. You are strongly encouraged to dive into these if you wish to find out more – you are bound to find some real gems of insights there. The vast majority of studies featured in this book have been peer-reviewed and subject to rigorous scrutiny from the academic community; the small number of pieces of research featured that haven't come directly from academia instead emanate from publications covering the very best of business thinking. Of course, any errors of interpretation lie entirely with this author.

How to read this book

Divided into three sections – *Ideas about people; Ideas about performance; Ideas about organisations* – this book can be dipped into and out of as you wish. In each chapter, you are presented with a summary of some of the key research undertaken on the topic ('What you need to know'), a synopsis of why this should matter to you ('Why it matters'), helpful tips for more effective ways of working ('How this will change the way you work') and some handy quotes that you can drop into your next office conversation and demonstrate your intellectual prowess ('What you might say about this'). Enjoy!

What you might say about this

'There's a whole world of incredible research out there that we need to bring into our day-to-day practical business thinking.'

'I now know a lot more about why best-laid plans often go awry – and I have some clever and innovative thoughts on how to stop this happening in the future.'

'The next time someone asks me "Where's the evidence behind your thinking?" I'll be able to provide them with it.'

Part 1

IDEAS ABOUT PEOPLE

IDEA #2
If you fear losing, you're more likely to lose out

We are naturally hard-wired to fear losses much more than we value gains – this can severely impair sensible decision-making in business.

What you need to know

Consider this:

You are offered a gamble on the toss of a two-sided coin.

- If you lose, you pay £100.
- How much would you demand as payment for winning to take the gamble?

What figure did you give? Most probably – like the majority of people offered this gamble – it was somewhere between £200 and £300. This means that you value avoiding losing around two to three times more than winning. This economically irrational preference has become known as 'loss aversion' – the idea that generally people prefer to avoid losses than gain profits. As the Nobel Prize-winning behavioural economist Daniel Kahneman and his research partner, Amos Tversky, pithily summarised: 'In human decision-making, losses loom larger than gains.'

Why it matters

Loss aversion affects every walk of life. One study – of more than 2.5 million putts at the PGA Tour – clearly demonstrated that even professional golfers demonstrate this fear of loss. The study found that golfers are significantly more accurate when putting for par (i.e., to avoid loss) than when either putting for over or under par.

In the business world, you don't need to look far for examples of loss aversion:

- Many investors sell stocks that have gained value too early because they fear losing what they've gained.

- Only a tiny fraction of people leave full-time employment to launch their dream start-up because they fear the loss of their steady income stream more than the potential future gains of their venture.

- Nobody ever sells insurance on the basis of what you *gain* by purchasing the policy – rather, they focus on what you're likely to *lose* if you don't take out insurance.

To mitigate the effects of loss aversion, you need to look out for your internal biases and those of your colleagues or customers. In the former, when evaluating any options, check if you are overvaluing a potential loss and undervaluing the possible gains at stake. In the latter, be sensitive to the loss aversion that others exhibit. When presenting options to an audience, for example, always bear in mind how loss aversion will affect how they perceive what you present – use our fear of loss to your benefit.

How this will change the way you work

- Loss aversion can make us emotionally attached to investments. The longer you hold onto something, the harder it is to sell – even if it is losing you money. Under emotionally neutral environments, create clear criteria for when you would sell an investment and stick to them when the losses begin to rack up.

- Trial your goods or services with potential customers. The moment your offering becomes part of their day-to-day lives, the more keenly they will feel its loss – and seek to avoid it. How often have you taken out a trial subscription with the intention of cancelling before payment started, only to fail to do so?

- Think about how you frame your messages with regard to loss aversion. What do you think would sound more compelling to a potential client: 'We can stop you from losing 10 per cent of your workforce' or 'We can keep your headcount figures steady'?

What you might say about this

'We need to pitch this investment carefully – on paper the potential gains are high, but the investors will overestimate the likelihood of us incurring losses.'

'Losing is no big deal – it's the price you sometimes pay for making sound decisions that just might not work out.'

'He's not being rational about his career prospects – I need to help him understand how he's being affected by loss aversion.'

Where you can find out more

Daniel Kahneman, *Thinking, Fast and Slow*, Penguin: Allen Lane, 2011.

'Is Tiger Woods loss averse? Persistent bias in the face of experience, competition, and high stakes', Devin G. Pope and Maurice E. Schweiter, *The American Economic Review*, February 2011.

Nassim Nicholas Taleb, *The Black Swan: The Impact of the Highly Improbable*, Penguin: Allen Lane, 2007.

IDEA #3
The hedgehog and the fox – why experts get it wrong

Knowing too much can make your predictions less reliable.

What you need to know

The ancient Greek poet Archilochus once famously wrote, 'the fox knows many things, but the hedgehog knows one big thing.' The philosopher Isaiah Berlin then appropriated this distinction to categorise great writers and thinkers into two camps: hedgehogs (such as Plato and Nietzsche), who see the world through one great big idea, and foxes (such as Aristotle or Shakespeare), who view it through multiple lenses. More recently, the Berkeley-based philosopher Philip Tetlock has used the analogy to explain the findings of his 20-year study of the accuracy of political forecasts made by 'experts'.

Tetlock analysed 82,631 forecasts made by 284 individuals specialising in 'commenting or offering advice on political and economic trends'. Faced with (then) contemporary questions on the likely outcome of issues such as the end of apartheid in South Africa or the chances of US military involvement in the Persian Gulf, the experts performed poorly. For each question the experts were given three possible choices: status quo to remain; more of something; or less of something. Compared with what then actually happened, they performed worse than if they had chosen their answers at random – they were correct far less than 33 per cent of the time. Dart-throwing monkeys, as the phrase goes, would have done a better job. Tetlock's research also made another important discovery. The more specialist knowledge an expert had on an issue (a hedgehog, in other words) the less reliable their predictions; the foxes performed better.

Why it matters

Tetlock highlights three likely reasons for this fallacy of expert predictions. First, there is no accountability for experts' forecasts. If a leading business guru appears on television and erroneously predicts economic growth for a certain sector, no one is likely to call them up on it if they turn out to be wrong. Second, experts frequently overvalue probabilities. Simple probability theory demonstrates that the likelihood of two variables occurring simultaneously (i.e., Spain's economy will stay in recession *and* the country will leave the Eurozone) is less likely to occur than just one variable – but experts usually add detail (and therefore variables to their predictions) to sound authoritative. Third, and linked to the second point, demand for forecasts in popular media focus on specific (and therefore less likely) predictions – vague claims that '*x* could happen, but you need to consider *y*, too' don't sound as engaging as '*z* is definitely going to happen'.

How this will change the way you work

- Remember when you hear a prediction that the more detailed it is, the less likely it is to happen. Economists famously recount the 'Linda problem' as evidence that individuals overestimate probabilities of events where there is 'plausible' detail. Consider the following statement: 'Linda is 31 years old, single, outspoken, and very bright. She has a degree in philosophy. As a student, she was deeply concerned with issues of discrimination and social justice and also participated in antinuclear demonstrations.' Is it more likely that Linda is: a) a bank clerk; or b) a bank clerk active in the feminist movement? Option a) is much more likely before there are fewer variables at play, but you probably said b) because it sounded more plausible. In short, expert economic and business commentators can give useful insights into the future, but their predictions are likely to be no better – or even worse – than yours.

What you might say about this

'Did you read her latest newspaper column about the future of emerging markets? It sounds authoritative but the likelihood of that scenario happening is pretty low.'

'Just because they're an "expert" doesn't mean they're a fortune-teller.'

'Don't talk rubbish. The truth is we don't know.'

Where you can find out more

Isaiah Berlin, *The Hedgehog and the Fox*, Weidenfeld & Nicolson, 1954.

Philip E. Tetlock, *Expert Political Judgement: How Good Is It? How Can We Know?*, Princeton University Press, 2006.

IDEA #4
How fortune favours the beautiful

Physically attractive people have tremendous advantages in life.

What you need to know

It probably won't surprise you to hear that attractive people get more breaks in life, but you may be amazed by the sheer extent of the benefits they receive through pure accident of birth. Daniel Hamermesh, a noted economist who coined the term 'pulchronomics' – the economics of beauty – has demonstrated that not only do attractive people earn more than their physically less attractive peers but they also receive milder prison sentences, get loans more easily, are more productive at work, are happier, and have more beautiful and better educated spouses. The financial implications of this are stark. An American worker with bottom-quintile looks (as judged by individuals selected at random) is estimated to earn $230,000 less over a lifetime than a similarly skilled worker judged to be in the top third of attractiveness, even after adjusting for education and other factors.

Why it matters

Luckily, for the less aesthetically blessed, intelligence is still the most highly valued skill in working environments. However a 2011 paper in *Psychological Science* uncovered a strong correlation between high financial performance in Fortune 500 companies and the width of their (male) CEOs' faces. Facial width-to-height ratio (WHR) has previously been shown to be a sign of likely male aggression (and attractiveness – the archetypal 'strong jaw'). In other words, males with wider faces tend to exhibit domineering and aggressive behaviour.

In business, the implications of beauty preference are complex:

- Individuals with similar qualities or qualifications can sometimes receive very different pay packages based purely on their appearance. One study of more than 400 economics teachers in Ontario found that those who had been considered 'hot' by their students (who voted on www.ratemyprofessors.com) were between 6 and 17 per cent more likely to earn more than $100,000.

- However, it's not always clear that this preference towards physically attractive people is commercially disadvantageous. Studies have shown that attractive people are more productive at work, are liked more by peers, and bring in more revenues than less attractive colleagues.

- While beauty is in the eye of the beholder, there is common consensus around who qualifies as 'attractive'. In one study, a group of individuals were assessed for physical attractiveness on a five-point scale by two different observers. Half of the individuals were scored identically and very few assessments had more than one point difference between the observers.

Some academics, such as Deborah Rhode, suggest the best way to mitigate beauty preference is to instigate legal protection for the physically less attractive – such as the Washington, DC municipal code against discrimination 'on the basis of outward appearance'.

Discrimination against race or sex is illegal, so discrimination against aesthetics should be too, the argument goes. For the time being though, how you approach this question in your workplace is a moral rather than a legal matter.

How this will change the way you work

- Beauty isn't something that can easily be changed. Thankfully, it's not the only valued workplace strength – emphasise other skills you have.

- Actively discriminating – subconsciously or not – in favour of beautiful individuals is a dangerous path to take, unless it is clearly beneficial to the job at hand. You would not discriminate on the grounds of race or gender.

- There are always exceptions to the rule. Beauty is a fortunate preference bestowed on some, but not everyone necessarily benefits from it. You therefore may want to be conscious about overcompensating *against* beauty preference.

What you might say about this

'People like working with attractive people. I don't think beauty preference is a big problem.'

'We profess to be a truly equal opportunities employer, but are we subconsciously discriminating against people because of their looks?'

'Intelligence is still more highly valued than looks. Beauty preference is just another one of those irrational preferences we need to be conscious of.'

Where you can find out more

Daniel S. Hamermesh, *Beauty Pays: Why Attractive People Are More Successful*, Princeton University Press, 2011.

'A face only an investor could love: CEOs' facial structure predicts their firms' financial performance', E.M. Wong, M.E. Ormiston and M.P. Haselhuhn, *Psychological Science*, Vol. 22, No. 12, 2011.

Deborah L. Rhode, *The Beauty Bias: The Injustice of Appearance in Life and Law*, Oxford University Press, 2010.

IDEA #5
When you can skip that meeting

How 'face-time' can help – and hinder – meetings.

What you need to know

A team of researchers from INSEAD and the Kellogg School of Management at Northwestern University conducted two meta-analyses to find the impact of 'being present' (i.e., face-to-face communication – either in person or via video conferencing) on the quality of outcomes for meetings, both in terms of decision-making and negotiations. Unexpectedly, and counter to conventional wisdom, it seems face-to-face meetings may not always be best.

Why it matters

Seeking to create a simple yet compelling model for their analyses, the research team discovered four surprising observations:

- When the individuals involved were previously unacquainted with each other, richer communication channels – such as face-to-face meetings or video conferencing – had a positive impact on the quality of outcomes for decision-making and negotiations. In this instance, being able to pick up nonverbal cues or tones of voice helped individuals to learn more about each other, and thus – we can hypothesise – establish trust and rapport more quickly, which facilitates better meeting outcomes.

- When the individuals involved already had good working relationships from previous interactions, the positive impact of richer communication channels over communication such as email or instant messaging was far less pronounced. Where cooperative relationships already existed, the mode of communication appeared not to matter with regard to the quality of meeting outcomes.

- Surprisingly, when the individuals involved were already well acquainted with each other but there were tensions from previous disagreements or conflicts, richer communication channels actually had a *negative* impact on the quality of meetings. Seemingly, the heightened sensory nature of face-to-face meetings or Skype calls can actually exacerbate the non-cooperative relationship legacies. In these situations, at-a-distance communication channels such as emails, or the use of a neutral third-party intermediary, may be best.

- Factoring in cultural differences, the researchers found that Eastern cultures – which have a predisposition towards team working (an 'interdependence preference') compared to Western cultures (which have an 'independence' preference) – were less strongly affected by richer communication channels. This was because the Eastern interdependence preference leads to a naturally more cooperative working style, thus largely neutralising the impact of richer communication channels.

How this will change the way you work

- There are few companies or industries that do not bemoan the preponderance of seemingly endless, overstaffed, non-value-adding meetings in day-to-day schedules. Travel to these meetings can often take far longer than the meetings themselves. With it now being easier than ever to find ways around being physically present at meetings, the question should be, 'when do I really need to show my face?' The INSEAD/Kellogg research gives some simple but compelling answers: if you don't know the individuals present, do your best to turn up or join in via video conference. If you do know everyone and you're on good terms, emails, conference calls or instant messaging might be just as effective. If you do know the meeting participants and you're on bad terms, be careful; being physically present might make things worse.

- In another piece of INSEAD research, academics found that mimicking the behaviour – such as gestures, poses or mannerisms – of your opposites can lead to better negotiation outcomes and mimicry is a powerful way of 'building trust and, consequently, information-sharing in a negotiation'. So if you do decide to turn up to a negotiation in person, consider copying the other sides' body language.

What you might say about this

'Let's just do a conference call on this – we don't need a full meeting.'

'We've never met these guys before; I think we should really make the effort to be present.'

'We had a really bad meeting last time and I don't want to make things worse. Let's try and smooth things out via email first and then reconsider where we are.'

Where you can find out more

'The communication orientation model: Explaining the diverse effects of sight, sound and synchronicity on negotiation and group decision-making outcomes', Roderick I. Swaab, Adam D. Galinsky, Victoria Medvec and Daniel A. Diermeier, *Personality and Social Psychology Review*, Vol. 16, No. 1, 2012.

'Chameleons bake bigger pies and take bigger pieces: Strategic behavioral mimicry facilitated negotiation outcomes', William W. Maddux, Elizabeth Mullen and Adam D. Galinsky, *Journal of Experimental Social Psychology*, Vol. 44, No. 2, 2008.

IDEA #6
How to improve your memory

Forgot something?

What you need to know

In recent years considerable research and development has focused on creating memory-training games and products that promise to lead to all kinds of personal improvement: from treating attention deficit hyperactivity disorder (ADHD) and dyslexia to even increasing IQ levels. Studies evaluating the success of these techniques have come to rather disappointing conclusions. For instance, while a game involving memory recall of certain patterns on screen may help improve your ability to recall patterns, this doesn't necessarily mean you will be able to remember your presentation on last year's financial performance better too. However, there is evidence to suggest that memory training can be helpful as long as it's linked to the specific skills you're seeking to improve.

Why it matters

With today's ease of connectivity and ready access to mines of information such as Wikipedia, the premium on having a good memory feels less great than ever before. Forgotten how to get somewhere? Look it up on your phone, on the go. Can't remember the technical specification of a product you're developing? A quick Google search will get you the answer. Yet there is a danger in becoming over-reliant on this work-around rather than actually bothering to remember things. When asked a question in the workplace, which is the more compelling answer: a) the actual correct answer, retrieved from your knowledge and personal experiences; or b) 'I can't remember, but I can find out in ten seconds from the internet'? Memory still matters and developments in memory improvement techniques have now made it possible to actually improve your recognition skills.

How this will change the way you work

An alternative to memory games is to give meaning to facts and figures you take in. Vicki Culpin, of Ashridge Business School, has devised a powerful mnemonic to help improve your memory recall: MARC. This involves the following process, to be undertaken when reading a financial report, for instance:

- **M(eaning)** – draw links between the new information you are acquiring and previous information you already know. For example, how does the financial information you are reading compare with that of competitors or historic performance?

- **A(ttention)** – retention requires focused and dedicated concentration. If you're reading the report while thinking about other matters, or listening to office conversations at the same time, you'll be unlikely to retain the new knowledge.

- **R(epetition)** – once you have learnt something new, try to recall it soon after to help solidify the neural links. Try to drop your new knowledge into a conversation with co-workers, for instance.

- **C(reativity)** – think of different and distinctive ways to remember your new information as distinctiveness will help in recall. If you're reading the information in an unusual place – on a plane, for instance – link the knowledge to this.

What you might say about this

'All I need to remember are the techniques for improving my memory.'

'If I'm distracted, I'm not going to be able to remember anything.'

'I'm impressed by people who have great memories – I'm going to work hard at becoming more like them.'

Where you can find out more

'Does working memory training work? The promise and challenges of enhancing cognition by training working memory', A.B. Morrison and J.M. Chein, *Psychonomic Bulletin & Review*, No. 18, 2011.

'From goldfish to elephant – make your MARC in business: Memory techniques', Vicki Culpin, *The Ashridge Journal*, Spring 2008.

IDEA #7
Nice gals finish last, nice guys aren't far behind

Disagreeable men and women earn more than their more pleasant counterparts.

What you need to know

A 2012 study in the *Journal of Personality and Social Psychology* analysed data on the careers of over 10,000 American workers' careers over more than 20 years to test the impact of their 'agreeableness' on their income earnings. The workers – from a wide variety of professions and ages – were asked to self-assess their 'agreeableness'; generally defined as the extent to which one is friendly or compassionate rather than cold or unkind. The researchers then controlled the results for factors such as education and job complexity that might introduce bias. The findings were startling: Men who were 'disagreeable' earned 18 per cent – or an average of $9,772 per year – more than agreeable men, whereas 'disagreeable' women earned 5.5 per cent more than their agreeable female peers – equating to additional earnings of $1,828 per year.

Why it matters

The findings from the research highlight three conundrums for the workplace:

- Disagreeable characteristics – commonly defined in personality research as the extent to which one is willing to forgo social harmony and the degree to which one is comfortable being critical of others – are seemingly highly valued in the workplace.

- Men who exhibit disagreeable characteristics benefit much more than women who do likewise – by up to three times as much. In a separate study, where 460 students were asked to act as HR managers evaluating short descriptions of candidates under consideration for a consulting position, 'disagreeable' men were clearly favoured for the position over 'disagreeable' women or 'agreeable' types of both genders.

- The findings of the study seem to reinforce gender stereotypes. Clinical or hard-nosed characteristics in men are favoured much more strongly than in women. This has a knock-on effect on likely incomes for men and women, and helps to reinforce gender pay differentials in business.

How this will change the way you work

- Find out if you're too 'agreeable'. The Big Five personality traits are commonly used in psychology to assess characteristic preferences (see Costa and McCrae, 1992), and a quick internet search will show you how to assess yourself. Alternatively you could ask others to rate you on 'agreeableness'. In the *Journal of Personality and Social Psychology* study, individuals were asked: 'How much do you feel that agreeable describes you as a person, where 1 means quarrelsome and 5 means agreeable?'

- If you feel your agreeable personality could do with some tweaking, there are a couple of steps you can take to change your behaviour. The first is to appreciate that there is a subtle but important distinction between being 'agreeable' and being 'respectful'. You can exhibit disagreeable characteristics – being challenging or critical – without being disrespectful.

- Next you can decide what to do – if anything. If you currently score high on 'agreeableness', reflect on whether you are too compliant with the plans and suggestions of others. If so, you may want to be conscious of opportunities for giving constructive feedback more often. Find a style that suits you; one that is firm without being aggressive. If you currently score very low on 'agreeableness', consider whether your behaviour may be having a negative impact on others. Ask them for feedback on this. It is highly likely that you can still be direct and effective while displaying more empathy than before.

What you might say about this

'He's too nice to succeed here. He needs to toughen up.'

'I know we think she's too bossy, but are we comparing her fairly when considering how we judge our male colleagues?'

'We shouldn't let disagreeable people get away with everything – we haven't found any evidence that being mean and hard-nosed actually makes you better at your job.'

Where you can find out more

'Do nice guys – and gals – really finish last? The joint effects of sex and agreeableness on income', T.A. Judge, B.A. Livingstone and C. Hurst, *Journal of Personality and Social Psychology*, Vol. 102, No. 2, 2012.

P.T. Costa Jr and R.R. McCrae, *The NEO PI-R Professional Manual*, Psychological Assessment Resources, 1992.

IDEA #8
People are terrible at fractions

Bad maths can lead to some ridiculously poor choices.

What you need to know

Special offer time! You're trying to get your supermarket shopping done in the fastest time possible. Nearly done, you just need to pick up a pack of breakfast cereal and are confronted with two offers for nearly identical products:

- 'Extra value time! Get 33 per cent extra cereal – free!'

- 'Discount time! We've knocked 33 per cent off our price!'

There's no difference, right? I'm afraid there's quite a major one. Do the maths and you'll find that the second offer is the much better deal; you'd need 50 per cent more cereal to match a 33 per cent price discount.

A team of researchers from the Universities of Miami, Minnesota and Texas A&M found such errors of mathematical computation in a number of experiments designed to test consumers' ability to compare discount offers. Not only did their research showcase consumers' inability to evaluate discounts effectively but it also demonstrated a bias towards 'bonus pack' promotions over economically equivalent price discounts. In one experiment they conducted in a small retail store in a large metropolitan area, 73 per cent more hand lotion was sold when offered as a bonus pack than when marketed with a price equivalent discount – after controlling for all other factors.

Why it matters

The authors hypothesise that such simple, yet commonplace, mathematical errors are part of an inherent human tendency towards 'base value neglect'. This supports the thesis, demonstrated by a growing body of evidence, that shows consumers have difficulty calculating changes expressed as percentages because they struggle to link the percentage change back to the 'base value'. Given the ubiquity of the use of percentages in sales, marketing and promotions, it's helpful to know what their actual impact is on consumers.

How this will change the way you work

- If you want to discount effectively, give freebies rather than price discounts. A 'bonus value pack' (of up to 50 per cent more of the product in question) offer is much more likely to spur consumption than a 'get a third off the price' discount. In short, keep the discount as simple to understand as possible.

- However, the implications of base value neglect needn't be confined only to sales and marketing. As the authors of the study suggest, public policy – among other walks of life – can also be informed by these findings. They posit that: '[governments could] accelerate the adoption of greener products ... if [they] communicate improvements in energy efficiency rather than the decline in energy consumption (e.g., a 50 per cent increase in miles per gallon of a car v. the equivalent 33 per cent decrease in its fuel consumption).'

What you might say about this

'I can't give you the 5 per cent discount on our proposal that you were looking for, but we can give you five days' consulting work for free instead.'

'Actually do the maths – the discount might not be as good as it sounds.'

'Never offer percentage discounts.'

Where you can find out more

'When more is less: The impact of base value neglect on consumer preferences for bonus packs over price discounts', Haipeng Chen, Howard Marmorstein, Michael Tsiros and Akshay Rao, *Journal of Marketing*, Vol. 76, No. 4, 2012.

Daniel Kahneman, Paul Slovic and Amos Tversky, *Judgement Under Uncertainty: Heuristics and Biases*, Cambridge University Press, 1982.

IDEA #9
Why diverse support networks are crucial for success

Looking back on successful careers, individuals overwhelmingly pinpoint their success as being down to the emotional support they received, rather than technical advice or training.

What you need to know

Researchers from Appalachian State University, Boston University and Boston College wanted to identify the factors that lead to truly exceptional career success. Choosing baseball as their test case (a team sport frequently deemed analogous to teams in large organisations – especially in terms of team size, hierarchical relationships, and the balance between individual and group performance), the researchers analysed the induction speeches of 62 players accepted into the Major League Baseball Hall of Fame – the pinnacle of baseball career success – between 1956 and 2005.

Analysing the content of acceptance speeches of inductees into the Hall of Fame was highly revealing. In 63 per cent of cases inductees emphasised the role of emotional support from friends and family as being key to their career success; compared to only 37 per cent referring to coaching or more practical help as being vital to their achievements. In the prioritised ranking of factors contributing to career success, the factors read (in descending order of importance): family; friendship; role modelling from peers; and coaching.

The research also found differences between the most exceptional baseball players (those inducted in the first ballot of voting to the Hall of Fame) and other Hall of Fame inductees (inducted in later rounds of ballots). Using this difference as a proxy for achievement (the former being the highest achievers) the researchers found that first-round inductees received help and support from both more people and people from a wider range of communities (i.e., outside of baseball), and received both more functional support (i.e., coaching) and emotional support (i.e., friendship) from their support networks than later ballot inductees.

This research supports other studies that have also demonstrated the power of strong social networks on health outcomes. For instance, studies have shown that in stressful situations blood and heart rate pressure increases less when people are accompanied by individuals they feel emotionally close to. A 2010 paper analysing data from 148 studies covering more than 300,000 people from across the world found that individuals with poor social connections (for example, few friends) had on average a 50 per cent higher chance of death in the following 7.5 years from the study than those with strong social ties.

Why it matters

Organisations place a great premium on personnel development and performance appraisals. These are almost uniformly viewed on an individual basis. Personal development is something that is commonly perceived to be in the gift of the individual in question; they must work on developing a given competency or gain experience in certain fields or sectors. Similarly, performance appraisals focus on an individual's achievements or misdemeanours over a given time period. The clear link between strong social ties and career and life success suggests the need for a much more rounded view of individual performance and development – taking into account the impact of those close to the person in question. Who an individual's family, friends, line manager, career manager, mentor and colleagues are will have a huge impact on their professional success.

How this will change the way you work

- Run a 'buddy' system in your organisation that pairs individuals who work in very different areas of the business and wouldn't normally be expected to interact a great deal professionally.

- Find a career mentor who works in a very different field or area from you. Their different perspectives will help to lift you above your day-to-day work and enable you to see the bigger picture.

- Genuinely prioritise friends and family – don't just say that you do. Not only are they the key to personal happiness but also they may well be crucial in facilitating professional success, too.

What you might say about this

'He's having problems at home – we need to support him in whatever way we can.'

'I don't want to spend my life just in the office – I want to spend time with friends and family.'

'I'd like a career mentor who knows nothing about my profession.'

Where you can find out more

'On becoming extraordinary: The content and structure of the developmental networks of major league baseball hall of famers', Richard D. Cotton, Yan Shen and Reut Livne-Tarandach, *Academy of Management Journal*, Vol. 54, No. 1, 2011.

'Social relationships and mortality risk: A meta-analytic review', Julianne Holt-Lunstad, Timothy B. Smith and J. Bradley Layton, *PLOS Medicine*, July 2010.

IDEA #10
When your gut instinct may be right

If you're going to go with your gut instinct, you had better have faith in your feelings first.

What you need to know

Researchers from Columbia University and the University of Pittsburgh investigated the relationship between trust in one's feelings and the ability to predict the future. In doing so, they found that where individuals had high trust in their feelings, they consistently and significantly outperformed individuals who had low trust in their feelings while predicting future events. In short, if you have confidence that your predictions are going to be right, they are more likely to be so.

Why it matters

Across eight separate studies the researchers asked more than 1,200 participants to make predictions about some of the following: the outcome of the 2008 Clinton–Obama Democratic presidential nomination; the box office success of movies; the winner of *American Idol*; fluctuations on the Dow Jones Index; and the weather.

Participants in the studies were emotionally stimulated into conditions of having either a) high trust in their feelings (HTF); or b) low trust in their feelings (LTF). Participants were asked to recall 'situations in which you trusted your feelings to make a judgement or a decision and it was the right thing to do'. The HTF group was asked to remember two such situations – fairly easy to do, and therefore presumed to engender a high level of trust-in feelings. The LTF group was asked to recall ten situations – far harder to do, and likely to lead to a decreased trust-in-feelings. When then asked to make predictions about the future, the difference between the two groups was stark.

When individuals were asked to make predictions about the weather in their local area, '54 per cent of participants with HTFs made the correct prediction, more than twice the proportion of participants with LTFs (21 per cent)'. Importantly, when asked to estimate the weather in far-away states the predictions were far less accurate, suggesting one must have a good knowledge of a subject *and* HTF to make a good prediction about the future. Such findings were replicated in the other studies.

How this will change the way you work

- The researchers hypothesise that this fascinating discovery – dubbed the 'emotional oracle effect' – can be explained by how people dive into their conscious and subconscious memory. When we have HTF, we are stimulated into accessing the 'privileged window', which contains vast amounts of knowledge in our memories that we have learnt over time. By recalling this information, we are able to accurately use it to make informed predictions about the future. However, when we have LTF, we lack the internal confidence to reach into our recollections and look into the crystal ball.

- The key lesson from this research would appear to be: if you know something about a given subject, try to stimulate yourself into a HTF situation (by remembering when you were recently right about something, for instance) and then make your forecast based on your recalled previous knowledge. It's likely to be a pretty good prediction.

What you might say about this

'The vast quantities of things we've learnt over time are stored deep down in our memory and if we can access them, we can use them to make sensible forecasts about the future.'

'How confident are you about your prediction?'

'You know this field well. You just need to trust your instinct and feelings.'

Where you can find out more

'Feeling the future: The emotional oracle effect', Michel Tuan Pham, Leonard Lee and Andrew T. Stephen, *Journal of Consumer Research*, October 2012.

IDEA #11
How good do you think you are?

The better-than-average effect and worse-than-average effect.

What you need to know

A large number of studies have consistently supported the idea that humans have a cognitive bias towards overestimating their own abilities and skills; from IQ scores to healthy living to happy relationships. For example, in a 2000 survey, 87 per cent of Stanford MBA students rated their academic performance as above the median – a clear mathematical impossibility! This bias appears to be most marked for unskilled individuals. The 'Dunning-Kruger effect' (named after the academics who uncovered the finding) notes that, for a given skill, low-competency individuals are particularly guilty of both overestimating their own level of skill and failing to effectively evaluate the skills of those more competent than them.

More recent research has added depth to the findings. Seemingly, for low-skilled tasks (or commonly undertaken tasks, such as ironing) individuals are more likely to underestimate others' competence than for higher-skilled tasks (such as juggling), for which there appears to be a greater tendency to underestimate one's own competency – known as the 'worse-than-average' effect. It should be noted that, to date, most studies of these biases have been conducted in North America. As such, there is a lingering question mark as to whether the 'better-than-average' and 'worse-than-average' effect varies from culture to culture. A study comparing the USA and Hong Kong suggests there is some variation, but the 'better-than-average' bias was still apparent from participants in both geographic regions. There is still much more work to be done in this fascinating field.

Why it matters

The need to effectively allocate tasks and resources in businesses is a vital requirement for any successful company. Executives and senior managers need to delegate tasks throughout their organisation in an appropriately distributed manner: delegate too challenging a task to one of your team and you run the risk of failure; delegate tasks that are too menial and you risk demoralising the workforce. The better-than-average effect highlights a potential explanation for 'control freak-ish' yet ineffective managers – they fail to delegate tasks because they believe no one else can do them competently, but they themselves are not particularly skilled at undertaking them.

How this will change the way you work

- *Recognise your biases.* Like all potentially detrimental cognitive biases, the first step to overcoming them is to recognise when they occur. When in your day job do you put yourself at risk of exposing and acting upon your biases? Could you be doing this when conducting performance appraisals ('I'd have done that better'); taking on workstreams ('it can't be that hard'); or when recruiting ('they're not as good as I was at their career stage'), for instance?

- *Reconsider your task delegation.* Are you appropriately sharing your responsibilities to your team? How are you doing this?

Consider drawing up a list of all the tasks you are accountable for, who is doing them (you or others) and what the rationale is for your delegation strategy. Have you been exposing your biases in your decisions?

- *Reappraise your skillsets.* The worse-than-average effect poses interesting career questions for individuals. Have you been selling yourself short in your aspirations? Do you sometimes consider that there are careers or tasks you 'wouldn't be able to do well'? What leads you to say this? Perhaps you are underestimating your skills in this area because you don't know enough about the practicalities of the tasks involved.

What you might say about this

'Not everyone can be better than the average (mean or median)!'

'Am I overestimating how good I am? What's the impact of this?'

'I've always thought I don't have the skillset to work in financial services, but maybe I just don't know enough about the sector.'

Where you can find out more

'Overconfidence and underconfidence: When and why people underestimate (and overestimate) the competition', D.A. Moore and D.M. Cain, *Organizational Behavior and Human Decision Processes*, Vol. 103, No. 2, 2007.

'Not so above average after all: When people believe they are worse than average and its implications for theories of bias in social comparison', D.A. Moore, *Organizational Behavior and Human Decision Processes*, Vol. 102, No. 1, 2007.

IDEA #12
The changing face of great working relationships

The effectiveness of leaders is determined by changing criteria in leader–member relationships.

What you need to know

A sizeable amount of research has highlighted the impact 'leader–member exchanges' (the relationship between a leader and those they manage – also known as LMX) can have on workplace satisfaction, cultural homogeneity (for example, positive LMXs can result in leaders and members sharing similar values) and task performance. Academics from Michigan State University went one step further in their analysis and asked, 'how do these relationships change over time?'

The academics examined the LMX relationship in a setting where 69 MBA students were 'leaders' of teams of four to five undergraduate students, competing against each other over an eight-week period. The set-up was designed to reflect real-life organisational team dynamics, where more experienced individuals (on average, the leaders of the experiment were 28 years old and had 4.5 years of work experience) are usually in charge of junior colleagues (whose average age in the experiment was 22 years old and had little work experience). Through the experiment the researchers were able to analyse 330 leader–member 'dyads' (relationships between one individual and another) as there were 330 individual team members.

Why it matters

The findings of the experiment make for fascinating reading:

- Over the eight-week period, the quality of the leader–member relationships improved over time. So if you're starting a new project or role and are worried your working relationships are currently a bit fraught – don't concern yourself too much. With time you should expect the relationships to get better.

- At the early stages of the relationships, leaders and members used different criteria to assess the quality of the LMX (with positive quality defined as both sides recognising each other's potential and describing the relationship as being effective). Leaders tended to base their assessments on how extraverted a team member appeared. Members, on the other hand, based their assessments on how agreeable the leader was.

- Later in the relationships, different criteria were used by leaders and members to assess the quality of the LMX, but this time there was greater convergence in criteria. Later on, performance was the biggest driver of relationship quality.

How this will change the way you work

Whether you are a leader or team member, this research has important implications for how to behave when seeking to create good working relationships:

- Initially, first impressions do count and these early assessments are not always based on particularly objective criteria. In the absence of a shared history or reliable indicators of an individual's performance, assessments about the effectiveness of a relationship may initially be made on interpersonal interactions. These might consider how chatty or sociable someone is (extraversion) or how trusting or cooperative they are (agreeableness).

- After time, relationship quality usually improves and is based more on how good we perceive someone's performance to be. This is reassuring, as judgements on people – in an ideal world – should be based on their competence, not their niceness. However, we all know first impressions can count a lot and we also know that good working relationships generally lead to team satisfaction and good organisational outcomes. Furthermore, we often may not get enough time in a role to really showcase ourselves at the height of our performance.

- So if you want to make a good impression, here's what you need to do: if you're a team member, be friendly and talkative; if you're a team leader, trust your members and showcase your good nature.

What you might say about this

'How are you getting on with your new boss? What are you basing your assessment of your relationship on?'

'I'm just starting off and I'd like to get to know everybody first in a relaxed social setting.'

'Don't underestimate the impact of simply being friendly to people.'

Where you can find out more

'The development of leader-member exchanges: Exploring how personality and performance influence leader and member relationships over time', Jennifer D. Nahrgang, Frederick P. Morgeson and Remus Ilies, *Organizational Behavior and Human Decision Processes*, Vol. 108, No. 2, 2009.

'Leader-member exchange, transformational leadership, and value system', Venkat R. Krishnan, *Electronic Journal of Business Ethics and Organization Studies*, Vol. 10, No. 1, 2005.

IDEA #13
When not to take an overseas assignment

Studies of CEO career trajectories show that those who work on foreign assignments take longer to get to the top.

What you need to know

Researchers from the Rouen Business School and IE Business School looked at the careers of the chief executives of the largest 500 European and 500 American companies, keen to explore the impact of international experience on their career development. On average, CEOs are appointed to the top job 25 years after the start of their careers. Yet for the 32 per cent of CEOs whose careers were analysed who had international experience, the average time from career start to chief executive was two years longer.

Why it matters

Received wisdom has it that diverse experiences are key to successful careers. This may well be true; the study does not suggest that international experience leads to worse CEO performance or shorter top job tenure. However, for one crucial factor that every ambitious individual values highly – time – it is clear that taking posts away from the domestic base of your company adds years on to your career path to the top. This supports earlier research that concludes the closer an individual is to the centre of a firm's social network, the faster their career progression. The optimum time, according to Hamori and Koyuncu, to take a foreign assignment appears to be right at the start of your career (e.g., within the first five years), and ideally, it should be for no more than one year.

How this will change the way you work

- *For organisations*: improve how you career-manage employees on foreign assignments. Ensure that while they are away from the home organisation, close links are maintained with them. Having a career manager at the firm's domestic base may help in this.

- *For employees*: beyond thinking carefully about when you choose to take an international assignment, make clear to your employers your concerns about being 'forgotten'. If going on a long foreign assignment, ensure you are happy with the long-term career plan your organisation has for you (and to start with, make sure you have one!).

What you might say about this

'What guarantees can I have that you'll view my career progression in our foreign offices in the same way it would be viewed in the home office?'

'I don't want to take any assignment abroad that is longer than a year.'

'I understand that there's a risk this will slow down my career progression, but I believe I'll value the experience of working in a different culture more than moving up the career ladder at the fastest pace possible.'

Where you can find out more

'Career advancement in large organizations in Europe and the United States: Do international assignments add value?', M. Hamori and B. Koyuncu, *International Journal of Human Resource Management*, Vol. 22, No. 4, 2011.

'A social capital theory of career success', S.E. Seibert, M.L. Kraimer and R.C. Liden, *Academy of Management Journal*, Vol. 44, No. 2, 2001.

IDEA #14
The virtues of exchanging favours

Employees who are generous in giving favours are also more productive.

What you need to know

Francis Flynn, professor of organisational behaviour at Stanford, wanted to investigate the impact of responses to an age-old workplace dilemma: should one consent to, or request, favours in the workplace? Analysing survey, productivity and quality data on the working patterns of more than 160 engineers at a large US telecoms firm, Flynn came up with an unexpected finding: 'employees may be better off in terms of both status and productivity if they increase the frequency with which they exchange favours with co-workers rather than worry about the extent to which such exchanges are balanced.'

Unsurprisingly, employees who frequently exchanged favours were those with enhanced social status (defined by responses to questions such as 'How well respected is this person at work?' or 'How much influence does this person exert over decisions at work?') What was less expected, however, was that employees who frequently exchanged favours were also more productive employees (defined by criteria such as jobs completed, hours worked, errors committed and percentage of deadlines met). The correlation did have an interesting nuance, though; for frequent favour-exchangers', productivity reached its zenith when the balance between giving and receiving favours was very slightly tilted towards giving. Too much giving resulted in a reduction in productivity.

Why it matters

Many people have hang-ups about if it is right to ask for favours in the workplace (believing that 'only I am responsible for my job') or assenting to requests for help ('it's their problem, not mine'), but Flynn's research suggests that the more you exchange favours, the more you are both respected and productive – a pretty good combination. Rejecting the possible hypothesis for these findings that those who exchange more favours are simply better at their jobs because they have more developed skillsets, Professor Flynn also controlled his findings for factors such as seniority, length of time in the job and education levels. The productivity boost for exchanging favours remained even after these controls. Flynn posits two possible reasons for this. First, as a result of frequent favour-exchanges, employees become efficient in helping each other out – a virtuous cycle is formed whereby the favour-exchange process is quick and doesn't take time away from one's own job. Second, trust is built up between employees who learn to tackle bigger and more intractable problems together. As individuals are increasingly willing to team up together to help each other out, seemingly many hands make light work.

How this will change the way you work

- *Don't be afraid to ask for favours.* It won't make you look foolish and may in fact increase your social standing. It certainly should help you solve your problem if you ask the right person.

- *Be generous with your time.* Helping others can give you insights into other areas of the workplace, which in turn may give you a more rounded understanding of where you work. The more you understand how things work, the greater the likelihood is that you will be able to know who to turn to when you face a problem you can't solve on your own.

- *Try to keep a healthy balance between giving and asking for favours.* Too much giving may reduce your productivity. Too much asking may lead to resentment or a feeling that you are constantly 'crying wolf'. Pick and choose when you exchange favours strategically, though make sure you do both frequently.

What you might say about this

'Can you help me with this?'

'Of course I'd be happy to help out.'

'I'd love to help out but right now I'm really crunched with this deadline. However I'd be happy to put you in touch with someone who might be able to help.'

Where you can find out more

'How much should I help and how often? The effects of generosity and frequency of favour exchange on social status and productivity', F.J. Flynn, *Academy of Management Journal*, Vol. 46, No. 5, 2003.

IDEA #15
Going on leave? Mind the career gap

Leaves of absence may harm your career prospects.

What you need to know

Michael Judiesch and Karen Lyness tracked the progress of nearly 12,000 managers at a financial services corporation in order to understand the career impact of taking leaves of absence. Of the managers surveyed, 523 took a leave of absence (around 90 per cent of these managers were female – most likely this was because of maternity leave) over a two-year period, with absences ranging in duration from a median of two months to a maximum of 18 months. On return from leave, the salaries and promotions of these managers were tracked for a further 30 months. Controlling for factors such as gender, age, education, seniority and length of tenure, the researchers found that the likelihood of being promoted during the period of investigation was 18 per cent less for those who took leave compared to those who didn't and the leave-takers earned around 8 per cent less too. Drilling down, while there were no discernible differences in the implications of taking leave as a result of gender or length of absence, frequency of absence did have a significant impact. The more leaves of absence taken, the greater the negative impact on promotion prospects and salary.

Why it matters

The researchers hypothesised two possible explanations for the penalisation of workers who took leaves of absence. First, that it demonstrated a lack of commitment to the employers and, second, absence results in a reduction in on-the-job skills. Regarding the first point, in a later paper by the same researchers, there appears to be some proof in the pudding – 24 per cent of managers who took leave for 'family reasons' left their employ after returning (compared to a 17 per cent turnover rate over the same time period for managers who had not taken leave). With the regard to the second claim, Lyness and Judiesch's research demonstrated that managers returning from leave received lower performance scores than those who had not taken leave. However, comparing workers with similar job performance ratings, those who took leave were still more likely to be looked over for a promotion and take home a lower salary than those who had not taken leave.

How this will change the way you work

In many instances, leaves of absence are beyond the control of workers – 70 per cent of the leaves of absence studied were for 'medical reasons'. Consequently, it seems grossly unfair that any employee should be penalised as a result. Some important points to note:

- Employers should be aware of the potential hidden punishment for employees who take leave. Of course, there may be some instances were excessive leave is taken because an employee is not committed to their job or instances were leave is simply unavoidable – such as maternity leave. The point is that employers should not take leave as a proxy indicator for performance; instead job evaluations should be based on actual performance, not the number of days off someone has taken.

- Employers should also go out of their way to help retrain anyone who has been on leave for a considerable amount of time – if performance is liable to drop due to a career break, this doesn't mean one should stand by and let it happen. Instead, organisations should proactively take steps to mitigate any detrimental effects leave has on performance when an employee returns.

- On the flip side, workers should be wary of the dangers of going on leave and make sure they are fully prepared and ready to go when they return to the office.

What you might say about this

'You can't say he's not committed to us just because he went on leave. Judge him on performance, not inputs.'

'I'm scared taking leave will set my career back – I need to make sure I'm fully prepared for work when I return.'

'Taking a leave of absence isn't ideal, but it's still better than a full career break in terms of future career prospects.'

Where you can find out more

'Left behind? The impact of leaves of absence on managers' career success', Michael K. Judiesch and Karen S. Lyness, *Academy of Management Journal*, Vol. 42, No. 6, 1999.

'Are female managers quitters? The relationship of gender, promotions, and family leaves of absence to voluntary turnover', Karen S. Lyness and Michael K. Judiesch, *Journal of Applied Psychology*, Vol. 86, No. 6, 2001.

IDEA #16
You are *so* clever! Flattery and the boardroom

Flattery and ingratiation are powerful – if often derided – influencing techniques.

What you need to know

A survey of 760 external directors from 300 randomly selected large and mid-sized US industrial and service firms sought to understand what drives career success in the boardroom (in this survey, career success was defined as an individual gaining multiple board appointments). James D. Westphal and Ithai Stern, from the University of Michigan and Northwestern University, respectively, were particularly interested in three behavioural traits exhibited in the director network – in other words, by directors towards their fellow directors. These were ingratiation (i.e., offering personal favours); monitoring and controlling behaviour (i.e., constructively criticising management proposals); and provision of advice and information (i.e., providing input on strategic issues).

Following the survey the researchers followed the careers of the participants for the next two years, focusing on when the respondents were nominated for directorships on boards where a fellow director sat on the nominations committee or was the CEO. The study found that, of the 760 participants, 169 received at least one appointment to be a director at a company where a fellow director was either CEO or on the nominations committee and:

- directors who exhibiting monitoring or controlling behaviour were less likely to gain a position on another board where a peer sat;

- directors who exhibited provision of advice and information behaviour received a small increase in the likelihood of a peer-based nomination;

- directors who exhibited ingratiation behaviour with peers found their chances of receiving directorship nominations increase by around 70 per cent;

- women or ethnic minorities were less likely to be appointed to a directorship on another board.

Why it matters

Not only does the study highlight the worrying injustice of the director-selection process but it also demonstrates the power of flattery. These directors weren't offering any particularly helpful advice to their peers, they were just demonstrating 'social influencing tactics that serve to enhance one's interpersonal attractiveness and gain favour with another individual'. You may think that this only applies when the flattery is sincere (think of the clothes shop assistants who say you look 'fantastic' in everything you try on) but research from Hong Kong University also suggests that the power of flattery – even 'when the recipient knows that the flatterer is offering an insincere compliment, presumably driven by an ulterior motive' – remains a powerful and effective influencing technique.

How this will change the way you work

- If you're running a director-selection process, check if there are any obvious connections between members on the nominations committee and potential candidates. Go through the given statements of rationale for appointments – are they really objective and evidence-based?

- If you're a board member, work hard to overcome any gender and ethnic minority biases. One hypothesis for the finding that flattery is a less powerful tool for women and ethnic minorities is that since the composition of most US boards is largely male Caucasian, flattery from individuals outside this demographic group does not quite chime with the norms of the dominant group. This might mean non-white male voices are less well-heard on director boards. Ensure key discussions and decisions take place in the boardroom – where everyone is equal – rather than in social settings where women or ethnic minorities are less commonly present.

- More generally, rethink how you influence. Do you prefer to be straight-talking and challenging, rather than flattering and charming? Do you sometimes find that your advice gets ignored? Perhaps you could inject a little charm and flattery into your messages so people warm to you (and your advice) more.

What you might say about this

'A little charm goes a long way.'

'Is flattery any more manipulative than other influencing techniques?'

'Don't be blinded by his flattery – is what he's saying actually valuable?'

Where you can find out more

'Insincere flattery actually works: A dual attitudes perspective', Elaine Chan and Jaideep Sengupta, *Journal of Marketing Research*, Vol. 47, February 2010.

'Flattery will get you everywhere (especially if you are a male Caucasian): How ingratiation, boardroom behavior, and demographic minority status affect the likelihood of gaining additional board appointments at US companies', James D. Westphal and Ithai Stern, *Academy of Management Journal*, April 2007.

IDEA #17
Avoid choice overload: 'keep it simple, stupid'

Making it simple to buy your products may be the key to winning more customers.

What you need to know

In 2000, the psychologists Sheena Iyengar and Mark Lepper published a now well-cited study about jam and choice. In a luxury Californian food shop, the researchers set up a display table with samples of jam for tasting. In one variant of the experiment, six different types of jam were available; in another 24 different types were laid out. Prospective customers, after sampling the jams, were then offered vouchers entitling them to a discount to buy the jam. Conforming to orthodoxy choice theory, more customers were attracted to the display table with 24 types of jam than the one with just six. Surprisingly, though, the display with fewer jams led to more sales: 30 per cent of the jam tasters at the display stand with six jams used their discount voucher for a purchase, compared to a paltry 3 per cent at the table with 24 jams. It seemed that too much choice led to fewer sales.

Why it matters

Some psychologists have called this paradox 'choice overload'. Too much choice, they argue, leads to fewer purchases, a decrease in customer satisfaction, and a reduction in a customer's strength of preference for a particular product. These findings have been used by various vested interest groups – notably the psychologist Barry Schwartz – to decry excessive choice in modern consumer society. Backing up Schwartz's arguments, a study by the Food Marketing Institute found that the average American supermarket in 2010 stocked nearly 50,000 products – five times more than in 1975. Consumer surveys by the Corporate Executive Board have also suggested that 'decision simplicity' – the ease with which consumers can gather reliable information about their choices and evaluate their options – is crucial in converting prospective consumers into actual purchasers. So, there is a strong body of evidence that suggests too much choice can put off consumers to some degree, but the exact impact of this is still up for debate. For example, the message that simple is best is not without its critics. A 2010 meta-data analysis article in the *Journal of Consumer Research* looked at more than 50 experiments into 'choice overload' and found no obvious correlation between excessive choice and increased consumer anxiety.

How this will change the way you work

- *Don't overload potential consumers.* Irrespective of whether or not excessive choice leads to *negative* consumer emotions, there is little evidence that excessive choice generates *positive* emotions. Given that offering many options to consumers is usually more expensive for producers (e.g., consider basic principles of economies of scale), it makes sense to focus on some choice, but not too much.

- *Make it easy to evaluate products.* Consumers want to be able to easily and reliably make informed decisions about their purchases. Many supermarkets offer 'price checks' in their stores to show how they compare against competitors. Such tactics help give consumers a quick way of doing just this. The key is to make sure the information you provide is reliable and not misleading. Consumers will be turned off very quickly by disingenuous comparisons.

What you might say about this

'Do we really need to offer 87,000 combinations of coffee?'

'Have we asked our consumers what they really want?'

'Consumers want to be able to compare our services against others – let's make this as easy as possible for them to do.'

Where you can find out more

Barry Schwartz, *The Paradox of Choice: Why More Is Less*, HarperCollins, 2005.

'When choice is demotivating: Can one desire too much of a good thing?' Sheena S. Iyengar and Mark R. Lepper, *Journal of Personality and Social Psychology*, Vol. 79, No. 6, 2000.

'Can there ever be too many options? A meta-analytic review of choice overload', Benjamin Scheibehenne, Rainer Greifeneder and Peter M. Todd, *Journal of Consumer Research*, Vol. 37, No. 3, 2010.

IDEA #18
Why we're anchored to what we know

Outside suggestions can have a huge impact on our understanding of the world around us.

What you need to know

Next time you have a spare moment, test two distinct groups of your colleagues with one of the following experiments:

- *Experiment 1:* guess (but don't calculate) the product of the following: $1 \times 2 \times 3 \times 4 \times 5 \times 6 \times 7 \times 8$

- *Experiment 2:* guess (but don't calculate) the product of the following: $8 \times 7 \times 6 \times 5 \times 4 \times 3 \times 2 \times 1$

Notice a difference in the responses to the two questions? When Amos Tversky and Daniel Kahneman posed these questions to two separate groups, the average estimate for Experiment 1 was 512; for Experiment 2 the average estimate was 2,250 (the correct answer is 40,320). Clearly the questions are mathematically exactly the same, so why such a huge discrepancy? The answer lies in a concept known as the 'anchoring effect'. This is where we are unduly influenced in our evaluations by information that we have recently acquired – and often we are especially swayed by the first piece of information we have obtained in a given logical sequence. For example, in the above experiment, the fact that either '1' or '8' come first in the series influences whether an answer errs towards either a lower or higher final product estimate. The number has 'anchored' us to a particular range on a spectrum.

Why it matters

Anchoring can be seen in all walks of life. Whether a house price or car price seems too high or too low or whether we think we are fortunate or not to have the jobs that we have are all determined by how we 'anchor' our evaluations relative to other factors we are aware of. To give another example, in one experiment students were invited to a 15-minute poetry reading given by one of their professors. Half of the students were told they would have to pay $2 to attend, whereas the other half were told they would be paid $2 if they attended – in other words two distinct 'anchors' were applied. The students were then told that the reading would actually be free to attend. Incredibly, when asked if they would still be willing to attend – this time for free – only 8 per cent of those who were initially told they would be paid to attend were willing to go, compared to 35 per cent of students who initially believed they would be charged to attend. The students' willingness to attend the poetry reading had been influenced (or 'anchored') by whether they would have had to pay or be paid to attend the first time around.

How this will change the way you work

- Awareness of the anchoring effect can open up a whole new world of opportunities in business. Where you place a product on a shelf, how you discount a product or how you evaluate an employee's performance will all be hugely impacted by the anchoring effect.

- One trick to help overcome this is, when you are asked for your evaluation of a given issue, consider 'what am I actually basing my evaluation on?' Most of the time our evaluations are – subconsciously or not – based on benchmarks or relative comparisons. For example, how highly you rate a colleague will often be based on how you compare them to either yourself or other colleagues – these will form your 'anchors'. Question whether these anchors are helpful or might be susceptible to bias and try to increase your awareness of what the impact of this bias could be.

- It is, however, extremely difficult to truly overcome the anchoring effect. Seemingly, we are even at its mercy when we are clearly making a joke. In one experiment, when negotiating a salary, individuals who started the negotiation with a joke requesting a ludicrously high salary received packages over 10 per cent larger than those who didn't make the wisecrack.

What you might say about this

'What am I comparing this to? What's my anchor?'

'When we're interviewing candidates we need to be careful we don't use the previous or first candidate as an anchor for our assessments. This is meant to be an objective process.'

'This investment looks good value compared to the other options on the page – but are these actually sensible benchmarks?'

Where you can find out more

'Judgment under uncertainty: heuristics and biases', Amos Tversky and Daniel Kahneman, *Science*, Vol. 185, No. 4157, 1974.

'Tom Sawyer and the construction of value', Dan Ariely, George Loewenstein and Drazen Prelec, *Journal of Economic Behavior & Organization*, Vol. 60, No. 1, 2006.

'Initiating salary discussions with an extreme request: Anchoring effects on initial salary offers', Todd J. Thorsteinson, *Journal of Applied Social Psychology*, Vol. 41, No. 7, 2011.

IDEA #19
The negative impact of the superstar

The presence of a superstar performer on a team may have a negative impact on the performance of others.

What you need to know

Between 1999 and 2010, Tiger Woods was the undisputed king of the golfing world; consistently the world number one and uniformly considered to be the superior of his competitors. A common sports and business shibboleth is that the presence of a superstar performer such as Woods encourages his competitors to 'raise their game'. Jennifer Brown, an economist at Northwestern University, tested this claim and surprisingly found the contrary to be true. In fact, analysing PGA Tour data between 1999 and 2010, Brown found that when Woods participated in a tournament, competitors shot on average 0.8 strokes higher (and therefore worse) than without him. This 'superstar' effect was highest among those higher-skilled players in direct competition with Woods. Seemingly, the clear skill gap between Woods and his peers actually led to reduced competitiveness, as opposed to greater competitiveness. Over this time period, Brown estimates Woods pocketed a handsome $6m in earnings as a result of the 'superstar' effect.

Ongoing research from Harvard Business School has drawn similar conclusions to Brown's (although others, such as two professors from the University of North Carolina have challenged Brown's findings). This research has suggested three mechanisms for this decline in competitor performance: a reduction in effort ('What's the point?'); increased risk-taking ('I need to do something amazing to win this'); and increase in cognitive errors ('I'm trying harder but I seem to be making more mistakes').

Why it matters

If the presence of overtly superior individuals in competitions can actually lead to a reduction in effort from competitors, we need to be careful with regard to how sporting analogies are translated into the workplace. Legal and consulting firms that adopt the Cravath System's 'up or out' policy (either progress quickly or find work elsewhere) predicate its use on the assumption that intense competition leads to great performance. However, this research suggests that, at least in the presence of true workplace superstars, performance may actual decline as a result. While this might seem counterintuitive in a business context, any sports fan will be aware of the dilemma that weak teams face when competing against clear superiors – should they conserve their effort for another day or valiantly throw all their effort at the challenge, despite a likely defeat?

How this will change the way you work

- *Align 'superstar' qualities with true virtues.* Companies that highly value only a small sub-set of skills are more likely to have clear 'superstars'. For example, if financial performance is the most highly prized outcome in a company, individuals who close the most deals or secure the highest returns are likely to be earmarked as 'superstars'. However these individuals may only be 'superstars' in the narrowest sense of the word; they may have poor interpersonal, customer service or team-building skills. If 'superstars' can actually have a deleterious impact on others, make sure it doesn't become a trivial label that is easy to achieve.

- *Move the superstars around.* Ensure that your highest performers move around the business a lot. Not only will they develop a wide-ranging understanding of how the company operates, any negative impacts they may have on particular teams will hopefully only be short-term and therefore minimised.

- *Spread the winnings out.* Brown's research is particularly focused on zero-sum rank-order competitions where there is a very clear winner. In the workplace, 'employee of the month' awards or ranked performance tables are manifestations of these types of all-or-nothing competitions. Avoid these by either making performance recognition team-based or make multiple awards available (i.e., best employee for customer satisfaction, best innovator, most efficient performer, etc.) so that there are many winners.

What you might say about this

'Team-based awards avoid some of the negative impact of competition in the workplace.'

'She's clearly the superstar in her cohort, but we need to make sure we recognise the good work of others.'

'Who are our superstars and what's our strategy for managing them?'

Where you can find out more

'Quitters never win: The (adverse) incentive effects of competing with superstars', Jennifer Brown, *Journal of Political Economy*, Vol. 119, No. 5, 2011.

'Field evidence on individual behavior and performance in rank-order tournaments', K.J. Boudreau, C.E. Helfat, K.R. Lakhani and M. Menietti, *Harvard Business School* (working paper), August 2012.

IDEA #20
The value of caring

How you can soften the blow of giving bad news to an employee.

What you need to know

You have a difficult piece of news to break to one of your team members: they won't be getting the promotion they have spent the last six months working furiously hard to achieve – and that they fully expect to get. In the language of the social sciences, you are about to 'breach a psychological contract' with the individual, but bad news is bad news – there's nothing you can do to make up for the disappointment the individual will feel, right?

Wrong, according to a study by academics at the London School of Economics and Political Science and University of Illinois at Chicago. Their longitudinal study of more than 150 office workers at three companies found that individuals who felt strong 'perceived organisational support' (POS) towards their employers (in other words, they believed the company supported, cared for and valued them) and had good relationships with their line managers, were both less likely to view an unmet expectation such as not getting a pay rise as being a 'breach of psychological contract' and, even if they did consider a given incident such a breach, they were less likely to feel a sense of violation and betrayal as a result of the disappointment, compared to individuals who experienced low POS towards their paymasters.

Why it matters

Disappointment and resentment are common sentiments in workplace environments and this is even more so during times of economic strain. Inordinate amounts of time and money are spent by companies trying to create 'shared corporate values' and 'positive working cultures'. Such exercises are not without their merits, but they obscure the fact that a few, vocal, discontented individuals can utterly undermine such efforts. In other words, if you want a positive working environment, you need to minimise negativity.

Research by Dulac *et al.* shows that one way to inhibit negative emotions following disappointment is to simply show workers that you care about and value them – although critically this must be done in some way in advance of the bad news. In this study, support was demonstrated towards employees in two ways: on an organisational level and an individual level. In the case of the former, this can be demonstrated through such things as sensible attitudes towards flexible working or childcare support. In the case of the latter, this involves managers really listening, engaging with and acting on the problems of those they manage.

How this will change the way you work

- It won't come as a surprise to hear the recommendation that you should 'value your employees'. The real issue here is, if everyone knows this is the right thing to do, why do so few organisations really do this effectively? One hypothesis could be that, while in principle caring organisational cultures sound like the 'right thing to do', in practice, there are not obvious benefits to putting in the considerable time, money and effort required to achieve this.

- The evidence presented by the researchers from the LSE and University of Illinois suggests there are clear corporate benefits to be gained from caring from employees: they'll hate you less when you have to disappoint them, thereby minimising the disruptive impact of disgruntled employees.

What you might say about this

'We're going through tough times but this doesn't mean that we should cut all the company benefits – the reputational damage that will arise from disgruntled employees in the long run will outweigh any short-term financial benefits.'

'What's actually stopping us from really putting in place a caring and empathetic corporate culture?'

'Promoting someone isn't the only way to show we care about them.'

Where you can find out more

'Not all responses to breach are the same: A longitudinal study examining the interconnection of social exchange and psychological contract processes in organizations', Tanguy Dulac, Jacqueline A.-M. Coyle-Shapiro, David J. Henderson and Sandy J. Wayne, *Academy of Management Journal*, Vol. 51, No. 6, 2008.

IDEA #21
Take every email with a pinch of salt

People are much more likely to lie via email than other forms of communication – beware.

What you need to know

A study by researchers from DePaul, Rutgers and Lehigh Universities found that not only are individuals more willing to lie in emails than other forms of written communication but they also feel more justified in doing so. In one experiment, 48 participants took part in a bargaining game commonly known as the 'dictator'. The participants (A) were told they had $89 to share with a second party (B) – who they would never meet – who had to accept whatever they offered. B was only told that the money for sharing was between the value of $5 and $100. It was up to the As to decide both how to share the $89 and tell the Bs what the value of the pot for sharing was. The As were divided into two groups: one group would use email in the process, the other would use handwritten letters.

Of the email group, 92 per cent lied about the pot size to the second party (B), compared to 64 per cent of the handwritten communication group. Not only were emailers therefore 50 per cent more likely to lie, they even felt more justified in doing so. When both groups were asked: 'How justified would it be if you misrepresented the size of your pot to the recipient?' (on a scale of 7 [very justified] to 1 [not at all justified]), emailers averaged 4.8 on the 7-point scale whereas the handwritten group averaged responses of 3.9. Additionally, the extent to which people are more likely to lie using electronic media as opposed to in face-to-face interactions has also been supported by other studies, as well as the degree to which individuals are more likely to send offensive messages (or engage in 'trolling') via social media.

Why it matters

The world has gone email mad. Around three million emails are sent every second. Our inboxes are inundated with emails, which we're instantly informed of via our smartphones, and the pressure to respond immediately is immense. Presumably, the rise of email use is based on the belief that it is a more effective way of communicating with people, but is this really true? You probably already have your own strong opinions on the matter, but the finding that people are more likely to lie in emails than in other forms of communication may give you some food for thought.

Happily, there is also research that suggests it may be possible to spot when people are lying in emails. Studies by Jeffrey Hancock *et al.* of Cornell University have shown that emails economical with the truth, 'produced more words; [produced] more sense-based words (e.g., seeing, touching), and used fewer self-oriented [e.g., "I"] but more other-oriented pronouns [e.g., "you"]'. Watch out for these tell-tale signs!

How this will change the way you work

- *Check your email motivation before hitting send.* Why are you sending an email rather than making a phone call? Are you trying to avoid confrontation or an inconvenient truth? Maybe you're planning on telling a little 'white lie'. Trust is key in business. Do you really want to undermine it, and use email to help you do so?

- *Scan for signs of lying.* If you get an email that makes you think 'why is this in an email?', read the text carefully. Does it seem a bit too long or too emotive or does the sender seem to struggle with writing 'I'? You might be reading a pack of lies.

- *Use the paper trail to your benefit.* It seems counter-intuitive that individuals would lie when there's an easy trail to check what they're saying, but then again individuals aren't always classically 'rational'. Keep a log of any emails you're sceptical about and, if appropriate, see if the story checks out.

What you might say about this

'Why did they put this to me in email rather than just tell me to my face?'

'I don't really believe some things in this email, but at least I have it in writing so I can check its validity later.'

'I want us to stop using email when a brief phone call will suffice.'

Where you can find out more

'The finer points of lying online: E-mail versus pen-and-paper', C.E. Naquin, T.R. Kurtzberg and L.Y. Belkin, *Journal of Applied Psychology*, Vol. 95, No. 2, 2010.

'Liar, liar, hard drive on fire: How media context affects lying behavior', Mattitiyahu Zimbler and Robert S. Feldman, *Journal of Applied Social Psychology*, Vol. 41, No. 10, 2011.

'On lying and being lied to: A linguistic analysis of deception in computer-mediated communication', Jeffrey T. Hancock, Lauren E. Curry, Saurabh Goorha and Michael Woodworth, *Discourse Processes*, Vol. 45, No. 1, 2007.

IDEA #22
Anger management: she needs it, he doesn't

Women are penalised for demonstrating anger in the workplace, whereas men are admired for doing exactly the same.

What you need to know

Victoria Brescoll of Yale University specialises in both fascinating and provocative research on gender stereotypes in business. In 2008 she published an article on the outcome of three experiments she conducted that demonstrated the extent to which, compared to men acting in the same way, woman are disproportionately penalised for showing anger in the workplace (in Brescoll's experiments this was demonstrated in terms of perceived competence and estimated deserved salary). By comparison, consider an infamous Stanford University study where participants were shown two different clips of then President Bill Clinton at the time of the Monica Lewinsky scandal. In one clip, Clinton expressed sadness and guilt regarding his behaviour. In another clip, he expressed clear anger at the existence of investigations into his conduct. Participants who viewed the 'angry clip' were more likely to suggest he should remain in office than those who saw the 'remorseful clip'. Seemingly it is perceived that, for men, anger is a sign of strength; for women – as Brescoll's research shows – it is a sign of irrationality and weakness.

Why it matters

Despite countless 'equal opportunity' laws and edicts, it would appear discriminatory gender stereotypes are still alive and well in the workplace. In a 2012 study, again led by Brescoll, this time the extent to which female CEOs were talkative, was also shown to be subject to stereotypical prejudices. In one experiment, participants were asked to assess the competency of four (fictional) CEOs on a scale of one to seven. The four CEOs, along with their scores for competency as assessed by the study participants, were: a talkative male chief (5.6); a talkative female chief (5.1); a quiet male chief (4.8); and a quiet female chief (5.6). Women, according to the study, were deemed to be most competent when they are quiet and least competent when they communicate lots. The inverse was the case for men.

How this will change the way you work

- *Acknowledge stereotypes.* Clearly, first and foremost, a more effective way to combat discriminatory gender stereotypes needs to be uncovered. Explicitly reminding employees of the existence of stereotypes can be helpful (though even this is fraught with potential pitfalls – see Idea #59). There are seemingly no quick fixes for this issue; long-term cultural change is needed.

- *Confront the issue head on.* In the short term, dealing with the realities of the problem may be the best option. Women, unfortunately, may benefit from recognising that displays of anger in the workplace – even if they are intended (consciously or not) to be displays of strength – are often received poorly, and considered a sign of weakness. Men, if they wish to be

Machiavellian about the issue, might consider that every now and again a flash of anger can be interpreted as a sign of power and conviction.

What you might say about this

'When was the last time I stereotyped someone?'

'Solve this riddle: "A father and son are involved in a serious automobile accident. The son is taken to hospital for an emergency operation while the father is in a coma. However the surgeon, on seeing the patient, replies: 'I cannot operate on him; he is my son.' How is this possible?" What does your answer tell you about gender stereotypes?'

'He's getting angry about the issue. He's not being firm, he's being irrational.'

Where you can find out more

'Can an angry woman get ahead? Status conferral, gender, and expression of emotion in the workplace', V.L. Brescoll and E.L. Uhlmann, *Psychological Science*, Vol. 19, No. 3, 2008.

'Who takes the floor and why: Gender, power, and volubility in organizations', Victoria L. Brescoll, *Administrative Science Quarterly*, Vol. 20, No. 10, 2012.

'Anger and advancement versus sadness and subjugation: The effect of negative emotion expressions on social status conferral', Larissa Z. Tiedens, *Journal of Personality and Social Psychology*, Vol. 80, No. 1, 2001.

IDEA #23
Why emotional inconsistency is the worst trait in a manager

'Schizophrenic' behaviour from managers arouses great anxiety in employees.

What you need to know

In a study of more than 340 police officers in the Republic of Slovakia, researchers found that the managers who have the worst emotional impact on their employees were those who combined 'socially undermining' actions (such as being critical or insulting) with supportive ones in a short space of time. The impact of these actions on workers were measured across five dimensions: a) self-efficacy; b) organisational commitment; c) actively counterproductive behaviour; d) passively counterproductive behaviour; e) and psychosomatic health complaints. The results showed that these five traits were most negatively affected when a manager or supervisor appeared to be delivering mixed messages of both hostility and support. Surprisingly, the researchers also found that when employees were going through difficult times, the impact of supportive co-workers trying to mitigate a manager's debilitating behaviour was negligible – a bad boss can cause irreparable harm, it seems.

Why it matters

Managers are constantly taught to give feedback in a way that balances both constructive criticisms with outright praise. Done well, this can be very effective but, as the research from Slovakia suggests, done poorly – in a way in which the criticisms can make employees feel socially undermined – can create confusion and anxiety for workers.

How this will change the way you work

- To avoid creating unnecessary emotional anxiety, allow a period of time to elapse between giving an employee conflicting pieces of feedback.

- If allowing this time-gap is not possible, one should always ensure that any praise or criticism does not veer into either a positive or negative extreme, because if contradictory feedback is necessary later, its potentially negative impact will be less if the emotional extremes aroused are minimised.

What you might say about this

'I've just had words with him for that substandard report. I don't want to create confusion by now going and patting him on the back and saying great job for his presentation – I'll wait a few days before I give the positive feedback.'

'Keep your emotions in check when delivering any feedback – good or bad.'

'You can't be everyone's friend if you're their manager.'

Where you can find out more

'Social undermining in the workplace', Michelle K. Duffy, Daniel C. Ganster and Milan Pagon, *Academy of Management Journal*, Vol. 45, No. 2, 2002.

IDEA #24
How to catch a feeling

Group dynamics affect how individuals feel, with repercussions for the workplace.

What you need to know

Does how you feel or behave in the workplace have an impact on the emotional state of others? A wealth of research based on 'emotional contagion' – how emotions are transmitted between groups and individuals – suggests it most certainly does. One highly cited study – using actors and business school students – undertaken by Sigal Barsade of the Wharton School concluded that positive emotional contagion in groups leads to 'less group conflict, more group cooperation, and more cooperative decision-making choices', with the opposite being true for negative emotional contagion. Another paper by Doug Pugh determined that, in service settings, customers can '"catch" the [feelings] of employees through emotional contagion processes'. In other words, if an employee were to act with kindness, friendliness and positivity towards a customer, the customer in turn would feel more positive as a result. Further research has reinforced this point, although with the caveat that disingenuous 'positivity' from employees can have a negative effect on customers.

Why it matters

How we act in the workplace – either as managers, peers or employees – has a huge impact on those around us. Whilst positivity cannot be learnt or enforced, we need to be conscious of our behaviour and its consequences on others. The simple mantra of 'service with a smile' has been strongly reinforced by this research.

How this will change the way you work

- Any team manager or leader should take great heed of this research. It won't be surprising to know that your positive emotions can transmit themselves to your team or peers, but perhaps more significantly, your negative emotions can do so, too. Given the accentuated power dynamics leaders hold, it is likely that the effect of emotional contagion will be multiplied.

- Anyone in a customer service position must be made aware of the power their emotions will have on those they deal with. If you want your customers to be happy, those who deal with them should be happy too.

What you might say about this

'I'm in a negative mood today – I need to watch out that I don't let this rub off on others.'

'A happy company has happy customers.'

'How can we create a positive environment in our organisation?'

Where you can find out more

'The ripple effect: Emotional contagion and its influence on group behaviour', S.G. Barsade, *Administrative Science Quarterly*, Vol. 47, No. 4, 2002.

'Service with a smile: Emotional contagion in the service encounter', S. Douglas Pugh, *Academy of Management Journal*, Vol. 44, No. 5, 2001.

'Are all smiles created equal? How emotional contagion and emotional labor affect service relationships', Thorsten Hennig-Thurau, Markus Groth, Michael Paul and Dwayne D. Gremler, *Journal of Marketing*, Vol. 7, No. 3, 2006.

IDEA #25
The antisocial network

Individuals who feel strong group connections have an unhealthy tendency to alienate and dehumanise those outside their groups.

What you need to know

While there's lots of evidence that individuals gain physical and psychological benefits from strong social ties, research has also shown that strong social connections can lead to 'connected groups' dehumanising and treating poorly those outside their connections.

A study by Adam Waytz of the Kellogg School of Management and Nicholas Epley of the Chicago Booth School of Business found that groups with strong social bonds have a predilection to dehumanise people outside their group. The study conducted four experiments: the first three found that when individuals were asked to think about people they were close to, and then asked questions about individuals outside their social circle, they were more likely to fail to attribute human qualities (such as strong mental capabilities or individual autonomy) to these perceived outsiders; a fourth experiment presented participants with photographs of the 9/11 terrorist attacks and images of purported terrorist detainees responsible for the attacks. In one group participants were paired with friends and asked questions about how acceptable they found the use of torture techniques in interrogations. In the control group participants were paired with strangers and asked the same question. When paired with friends, participants were significantly more willing to dehumanise the detainees and endorse harming them through torture than when paired with strangers.

Why it matters

The business world commonly revolves around team environments or insider–outsider relationships. In the external consultant–client relationship, complaints are commonly heard by clients who feel that consultants patronise them or do not understand their problems. Recently merged organisations often struggle to assimilate new teams into joint working partnerships. In highly competitive organisations, it is often believed that creating rival team dynamics can help to drive up performance. This research suggests that this may well come at the expense of fostering collaborative environments.

How this will change the way you work

- Keep team dynamics fresh by continuously rotating members. This will help inject new perspectives into the team and stop them from becoming alienated from other teams.

- Stop yourself if you ever find yourself uttering the phrase to your team about another group of individuals: 'I don't understand what their problem is – they just don't get it.' It could be that your team is the problem, rather than the other way around.

- Ask people outside your immediate social network for their thoughts on workplace issues. If you keep on asking your team members for advice, you may end up creating an unhelpful 'silo mentality'.

What you might say about this

'They don't think or act like us.'

'Let's put ourselves in their situation.'

'Team spirit is great, but we shouldn't let ourselves become alienated from the rest of the organisation.'

Where you can find out more

'Social connection enables dehumanization', Adam Waytz and Nicholas Epley, *Journal of Experimental Social Psychology*, Vol. 48, No. 1, 2012.

IDEA #26
Why being boring can make you a brilliant CEO

Dullness and diligence trump charisma and charm as great qualities to look for in a CEO.

What you need to know

With top management pay inexorably on the rise, 'what makes a great CEO?' is a multi-million dollar question. In a detailed study of 316 candidates under consideration to be CEOs of companies undergoing private equity transactions during the period 2000 to 2006, researchers concluded that, for both buyout and venture capital CEOs, 'success is more strongly related to execution and resoluteness skills than to [communication or] interpersonal-related skills'. In other words, CEOs who excelled at detail and getting stuff done outperformed those who had good listening, team-building or oratorical skills. In an earlier study, academics from Yale University and the University of Pittsburgh came to a similar conclusion when analysing the performance of 128 CEOs at major US companies. They found that 'organizational performance is associated with subsequent perceptions of CEO charisma, but that perceptions of CEO charisma are not associated with subsequent organizational performance, even after incorporating the potential moderating effect of environmental uncertainty'. In other words, people often assume great companies must have charismatic CEOs, but there is no causal link that conclusively proves charismatic CEOs drive up company performance.

Why it matters

It seems that, while it's easy to assume great-performing firms have great leaders, this may in fact be nothing more than a variation of the 'halo effect' (see Idea #33). True value-adding from CEOs comes in the tireless execution of strategy, hard work and attention to detail. In a survey of business leadership throughout the twentieth century, researchers from Michigan State University similarly concluded that 'conscientiousness is a valid predictor across performance measures [for both CEOs and other occupations]'. The devil, it would appear, is in diligent execution of the detail.

How this will change the way you work

Charisma and flamboyance have long been regarded as attractive traits in any leader. The ability to inspire others, to engage and motivate them, are commonly portrayed in every heroic team story – be it sporting success, corporate greatness or military bravery – as prerequisite characteristics of the great leaders of these fables, but the evidence, on closer inspection, does not back up the hypothesis that these character traits are what make great business leaders. If you think you're too dull to get to the top, or too devoted to precision, think again. Really great CEOs make an impression through their actions, not their words.

What you might say about this

'I hear people say, "he can really command a room" and so he's destined for the top. I don't really buy that logic. He'll get to the top if he's good at execution of the detail.'

'He's too flash – I want somebody who gets stuff done, not somebody who poses for the cameras.'

'Being a great team player doesn't necessarily make you a great team leader.'

Where you can find out more

'Which CEO characteristics and abilities matter?', Steven N. Kaplan, Mark M. Klebanov and Morten Sorensen, *The Journal of Finance*, Vol. 67, No. 3, 2012.

'Does CEO charisma matter? An empirical analysis of the relationships among organizational performance, environmental uncertainty, and top management team perception of CEO charisma', Bradley R. Agle, Nandu J. Nagarajan, Jeffrey A. Sonnenfeld and Dhinu Srinivasan, *Academy of Management Journal*, Vol. 49, No. 1, 2006.

'Personality and performance at the beginning of the new millennium: What do we know and where do we go next?', Murray R. Barrick, Michael K. Mount and Timothy A. Judge, *Personality and Performance*, Vol. 9, No. 1/2, 2001.

IDEA #27
How to tell if a leader is lying

Lots of superlatives and talk of 'the team' – you might be listening to a lie.

What you need to know

Analysing nearly 30,000 transcripts of conference calls led by American CEOs or CFOs held between 2003 and 2007, David Larcker and Anastasia Zakolyukina of Stanford's Graduate School of Business may have found the tell-tale signs of lying leaders. Analysing the utterances of leaders in the conference calls when discussing company profits who later 'materially restated' their financial position (and using this chain of events as a proxy for potential fibbing) the professors noted two linguistic traits that may be clues to an untruthful earnings report from a leader. First, CEOs or CFOs whose companies revised their financial position were more likely to use terms in the abstract third person when referring to their firms. Thus phrases like 'the company' and 'the team' were more likely to be used than 'I' and 'we'. Seemingly, fibbers prefer to distance themselves psychologically from their organisations. Second, lying leaders displayed a preference for exuberantly positive terms: 'fantastic' would replace 'good', for instance. Bombastic claims appear to be used to help mask untruths.

Significantly, the authors note some limitations of their report; the analytical model they used to analyse the transcripts are 4–6 per cent better than a random guess – good, but not definitive. Also the authors were unable to differentiate between leaders who were consciously lying and those who may have believed themselves to be speaking with genuine accuracy at the time, yet time's progression proved them wrong. Nonetheless, it would appear that they have uncovered some helpful verbal clues to listen out for.

Why it matters

If a company is a human body, CEOs – and to a lesser extent CFOs – are very explicitly the mouth (if nothing else). Investors hang on every word CEOs state publicly, looking for clues to the corporate strategy that might give them an edge in their decisions. Regulators, too, need to pay attention to what business leaders say, and whether their pronouncements are plausible. Coupled with research from Columbia University suggesting that powerful people are better liars, any verbal clues that can be offered to know when a business leader is lying are vital pieces of information that should not be ignored.

How this will change the way you work

Perhaps the greatest beneficiaries from this research will be business PR gurus and executives with something to hide. For them, if they're planning on telling a fib, the message is clear:

- Don't overdo it (i.e., financial performance isn't 'fantastic' – rather, it's 'healthy').
- Don't distance yourself from your firm (i.e., 'the market' isn't showing that 'the company' is doing well – rather, 'I' believe that 'we're' doing well).

What you might say about this

'I want to sound sincere, so I'm just going to keep it simple: "I'm really proud of the results we've posted."'

'She's using extremely glowing language about the company … is she trying to hide something?'

'Keep it plain and simple, stupid.'

Where you can find out more

'Defend your research: powerful people are better liars', Dana Carney, *Harvard Business Review*, May 2010.

'Detecting deceptive discussions in conference calls', David F. Larcker and Anastasia A. Zakolyukina, *Journal of Accounting Research*, Vol. 50, No. 2, 2012.

IDEA #28
Your willpower levels are precious and finite

Decision fatigue is a real and dangerous problem.

What you need to know

Research into more than 1,000 parole board decisions in Israel demonstrated the potentially devastating impact of exhausting our 'willpower' (a process also known as 'decision fatigue'). In around one-third of cases, parole for prisoners was approved, but the fluctuation of the variation in parole decisions was staggering. Prisoners appearing early in the morning received parole in around 70 per cent of instances, compared to only 10 per cent of prisoners appearing before the board in the evening. Analysing the judges' food-eating habits, a worrying relationship arose pointing to disproportionately higher numbers of parole grants being given shortly after food breaks. As the authors concluded, 'judicial rulings can be swayed by extraneous variables [such as when food is consumed] that should have no bearing on legal decisions'.

Why it matters

One hypothesis for this shocking finding is the concept of 'ego' or 'decision fatigue' forwarded by psychologist Roy Baumeister and science columnist John Tierney. They suggest that willpower – which is needed for decision-making – is like a muscle; used frequently it can become tired and depleted, leading to 'ego fatigue', which subsequently impairs decision-making. Willpower helps us in all manner of situations, from being able to exercise restraint and self-control when dieting, for instance, to controlling and mediating our thoughts and emotions – when it becomes depleted, it can cause us to lose self-control.

How this will change the way you work

- Willpower needs fuel to survive, and this takes the form of glucose. When decision fatigue sets in, glucose levels decrease. What we eat can have a big impact on the moderation of our willpower levels. Foods that convert into glucose quickly (such as sugary snacks or white bread) can lead to fluctuations in our glucose levels, whereas slow conversion foods (such as nuts or raw fruit) provide a lower but more stable release of glucose.

- Sleep is also vital in restoring willpower. However, trying to get a good night's sleep and eating well is clearly only part of the battle. You need to carefully moderate when and how many big decisions you make during the day, otherwise you risk suffering from 'ego fatigue' and hence poor decision-making.

What you might say about this

'Let's remove trivial decisions from the meeting agenda – we need to save people's energy for the really tough questions.'

'I get so tired from work but my job is really sedentary – I use up my energy making tough decisions.'

'Get some healthy snacks for the meeting containing natural sugars such as fruit – this will help perk people up and ensure glucose levels are released in a stable manner. Healthy snacks in meetings help in making sensible decisions.'

Where you can find out more

Roy F. Baumeister and John Tierney, *Willpower: Rediscovering the Greatest Human Strength*, Penguin, 2012.

'Extraneous factors in judicial decisions', Shai Danziger, Jonathan Levav and Liora Avnaim-Pesso, *Proceedings of the National Academy of Sciences*, Vol. 108, No. 17, 2011.

IDEA #29
The optimistic salesperson

Great salespeople are optimistic people.

What you need to know

Great salespeople come in all shapes and sizes. Despite the obvious commercial benefits of finding an answer, it has proved enduringly difficult to pin down the particular character traits that make some people better at selling than others – with the exception of one. In the late 1990s, Peter Schulman of the Wharton School published a fascinating paper on insurance sales teams that honed in on a specific characteristic that might be the key to successful salespeople: optimism. Schulman's study found that optimistic insurance salespeople sold on average 35 per cent more than pessimistic ones, and pessimistic ones were far more likely to quit their sales positions within the first year of taking up their jobs. Schulman's findings backed up the theory of the great salesman espoused in David Mayer and Herbert Greenberg's seminal paper from 1964, 'What makes a good salesman', which posited that empathy and ego drive (the latter of which ultimately requires great optimism, as one needs to continuously pick oneself up from disappointment) were common to all great salespeople.

Why it matters

As Philip Delves Broughton correctly notes, there is a strange attitude towards sales in business; an attitude that treats selling as a dirty word, almost on the borderline of that which is morally acceptable. As such, very little rigorous research has been dedicated to really understanding – in a truly evidence-based way – how to become a great salesperson. The suggestion that any selling tools or techniques are only secondary to the personal characteristic trait of optimism is reassuring, because as former president of the American Psychological Association, Martin Seligman, claimed, very popularly – optimism really can be learnt.

How this will change the way you work

Seligman built on the great psychologist Albert Ellis' work to develop the 'ABCDE model' for how to 'learn optimism'. When an individual experiences a pessimistic thought, the theory goes that they should talk through the model, which covers: Adversity; Beliefs arising; Consequences of the beliefs; Disputation of the beliefs; and Energisation as a result of successful disputation. For example:

- *Adversity*: 'I really flunked that job interview.'

- *Beliefs*: 'I'm bad at interviewing. I always have been, and as a result, I'm never going to get the job I want.'

- *Consequences*: you hold back from applying for future jobs in a position you really want and your fears about your interview performance compound themselves.

- *Disputation*: 'My interview wasn't that bad and there were lots of good candidates who also didn't get the post. I haven't interviewed for a very long time and I was probably a bit rusty; if I practise more next time I'll stand a much better chance. I got very helpful feedback from the interview, which means I know where to prioritise my efforts in preparation for next time.'

- *Energisation*: 'I know what I need to do to be successful in my next interview and I'm committed to doing it.'

What you might say about this

'A positive outlook and a willingness to pick yourself up and try again is worth more than any MBA.'

'We should test for optimism in our recruitment interviews for salespeople.'

'You can learn optimism – it's as easy as ABCDE.'

Where you can find out more

Philip Delves Broughton, *Life's a Pitch: What the World's Best Sales People Can Teach Us All*, Portfolio Penguin, 2012.

Martin E.P. Seligman, *Learned Optimism: How to Change Your Mind and Your Life*, Vintage Books, 2006.

'Applying learned optimism to increase sales productivity', Peter Schulman, *Journal of Personal Selling and Sales Management*, Vol. 19, No. 1, 1999.

IDEA #30
Stress leads to poor decision-making

Be careful when making decisions while under pressure or stressed.

What you need to know

For some time neuroscientists have been able to demonstrate that when we are under stress our decision-making skills are compromised. In a 1987 study of more than 100 men and women, individuals exposed to stress 'showed a significant tendency to offer solutions [to decision problems on a computer] before all available alternatives had been considered and to scan their alternatives in a non-systematic fashion [compared to] participants who were not exposed to stress'. In other words, under stress, the individuals jumped to conclusions and lacked logical thinking when searching for solutions.

More recent research from Utrecht University has pointed to similar conclusions (in this experiment individuals under stress were more likely to take unwise and risky decisions) and this study also suggested that the hormone cortisol may be the key variable that impairs decision-making. Intriguingly, however, cortisol appeared to affect men and women differently. For the former, high cortisol levels led to poor risk-taking decisions; for the latter, low cortisol levels led to poor risk-taking decisions.

Why it matters

In an age of constant communication and an 'always-on-the-job' mentality (see Idea #48), it's no wonder that surveys of stress levels have demonstrated a clear upwards trend. In 2010, a survey by the American Psychological Association found that 75 per cent of respondents felt their stress levels were so high they were having an impact on their health. Combine this with the relentless barrage of communication media and on-the-spot decisions managers need to make, the news that stress and good decision-making are poor bedfellows is cause for concern.

How this will change the way you work

- So how can you combat stress? In 1975 the Harvard-based physician Herbert Benson and Miriam Klipper wrote the popular self-help book, *The Relaxation Response*. Benson and Klipper expounded on a simple – yet clinically proven – method for reducing stress: deep breathing. Deep, abdominally centred breathing has been shown to affect the heart, brain, digestive and immunological systems.

- To put their findings into practice, first work out what are the warning signs that you feel stressed – usually these are things like increased heart rate, unpleasant stomach feelings or headaches.

- Then start some relaxation techniques. Find a quiet room on your own. Sit comfortably. Take deep, long breaths. Close your eyes and focus on just one word as you breathe. Repeat the word in your head over a ten-minute period, with your eyes closed and focused on your deep breathing. You should feel your stress levels diminish, which will put you in a better position to face those tough decisions ahead.

What you might say about this

'I'm going to start keeping a diary of how I feel so I can work out what are the tell-tale signs of me feeling stressed.'

'Relax. Take a deep breath.'

'I need some time on my own to de-stress. I should find a suitable room or location I can use, away from prying eyes.'

Where you can find out more

'Decision making under stress: Scanning of alternatives under controllable and uncontrollable threats', Giora Keinan, *Journal of Personality and Social Psychology*, Vol. 52, No. 3, 1987.

'Stress and decision-making in humans: Performance is related to cortisol reactivity, albeit differently in men and women', Ruud van den Bos, Marlies Harteveld and Hein Stoop, *Psychoneuroendocrinology*, Vol. 34, No. 10, 2009.

Herbert Benson and Miriam Z. Klipper, *The Relaxation Response*, HarperTorch, 1975.

IDEA #31
To opt in or opt out?

Simply changing the default setting of things has a big impact on how people behave.

What you need to know

Over the past decade or so, interest from both public and private sectors has developed in the field of 'nudge theory'. One of the early studies that really brought to light the possibilities of this field was Brigitte Madrian and Dennis Shea's investigation into enrolment rates in 401(k) – tax-deferred, often employer-matched – retirement savings plans at a large US corporate firm. The intriguing development that Madrian and Shea were concerned with was the introduction of 'auto-enrolment' in the 401(k) plan for employees at the firm. Employees were immediately enrolled in the programme by their employer, but then offered the opportunity to 'opt out'.

While enrolment rates for workers varied greatly by length of tenure, gender and other demographic factors, for new employees with less than five years' tenure, enrolment rates were around 50–65 per cent. However, post the change to an 'opt out' automatic enrolment system, participation rates for new employees rose to a staggering 86 per cent. By all accounts, saving for retirement is both a uniformly sensible thing to do and – given the difficulty people have with prioritising long-term decisions over short-term ones (see Idea #58) – a tricky thing to coerce individuals into doing. This was a remarkable and novel way to solve the problem.

Why it matters

Proponents of 'nudge theory' such as Cass Sunstein and David Thaler have found themselves at the forefront of avant-garde government policy-making in the USA, Denmark, France and, in particular, Britain in recent years. In Denmark, the 'opt out' system has been suggested as a means to increase organ donation rates, with plans being proposed to change to a system whereby the 'default' status for those taking out driving licences will be to consent to organ donation. Citizens will be allowed to opt out of this status, but by changing the social norms of what is expected it is anticipated the number of organ donors will rise substantially.

How this will change the way you work

- Even with rapid advances in technological development, the vast majority of business decisions are still ultimately governed by human interactions and behaviours. As a result, managers and leaders need to know how to make people change their behaviours, but to do so in a way that doesn't feel explicitly coercive or is likely to engender harmful ill feeling.

- One option may well be to adopt an 'opt out' approach to issues. Let's say that in a monthly meeting you run, you're finding it tricky to get people to vote on certain issues and thus get decisions through. Rather than pose a question, such as 'Today we need to decide on the bonus pot for the forthcoming quarter – what are people's thoughts on this?', you could go for an 'opt out' approach. For example: 'I've brought to today's meeting a proposal that this quarter's bonus pot should remain flat from the previous quarter. I've outlined the reasons why in this report. Unless anyone has any objections, I move that we vote this through. Do I hear any objections?' Here, the 'default' position is to adopt your recommendations and you have assumed that everyone will opt in. They may still choose to opt out – and this may still be the right thing – but by framing things so that what you've proposed is the norm, you're giving yourself a better chance of getting your plans through.

What you might say about this

'You know those boxes as the bottom of messages that say "Untick here to unsubscribe from this mailing list?" That's a perfect example of "nudge theory".'

'Unless I hear otherwise, from now on I'm going to assume you *are* attending the meeting.'

'We're going to automatically donate 0.5 per cent of your bonus to charity, unless you tell us otherwise.'

Where you can find out more

'The power of suggestion: Inertia in 401(k) participation and savings behavior', Brigitte C. Madrian and Dennis F. Shea, *Quarterly Journal of Economics*, Vol. 116, No. 4, 2001.

'Empirically informed regulation', Cass R. Sunstein, *The University of Chicago Law Review*, Vol. 78, No. 4, 2011.

IDEA #32
Rational man is dead. Salute the animal spirit

Standard economic theory has been blown apart by the reality of our animal spirit.

What you need to know

The Nobel-laureate economist George Akerlof and Yale professor Robert Shiller began writing their lament of classical economists' concept of the world in 2003 and, by the time they came to publish *Animal Spirits* in 2009 in the wake of the 2008 financial crises, their timing could not have been better. Their thesis builds upon John Maynard Keynes' observation in his 1936 book *The General Theory* that how humans really behave cannot be standardised into simple formulae and models, because 'our decisions to do something positive ... can only be taken as the result of animal spirits – a spontaneous urge to action rather than inaction, and not as the outcome of a weighted average of quantitative benefits multiplied by quantitative probabilities'. According to Akerlof and Shiller, since the Keynesian revolution, the role of emotionality in decision-making has been progressively sidelined in orthodox economic theory – much to the detriment of the discipline. For economics to be truly useful to the world, we need to bring emotion back into the equation.

Why it matters

Akerlof and Shiller identify five classes of spirit that substantially alter man's propensity to behave in entirely rational ways. These are:

1. *Confidence.* Negative or positive emotions can spiral in magnitude and erode rational decision-making; thus a trader who makes big gains one week becomes more confident they can repeat their performance the following week, despite much evidence that probability-wise this is highly unlikely.

2. *Fairness.* Individuals are highly attuned to what is fair or not – even if it goes against their best interests (and therefore their assumed 'rational behaviour').

3. *Corruption.* Power and money corrupts individuals and classical economics does not take enough account of these deviations from rational behaviour.

4. *Money illusion.* People are very bad at factoring in the effects of inflation into their financial calculations, which can lead to some perverse decision-making.

5. *Stories.* Narratives play much more powerfully to the memory than cold hard facts or figures (see Idea #65).

We need to consider these five spirits in tandem with any other assumptions we make about how we can 'expect' people to behave.

How this will change the way you work

- *Remember the spirits.* When trying to make predictions about how individuals will react to a given scenario (i.e., bringing a product to market, offering a redundancy package or changing subscription rates for a service) always bear in mind Akerlof and Shiller's five spirits. It might be simple to predict what will happen based on the assumption that people will always choose what is in their rational, best interest, but what if you complicate (and make more real) the issue by factoring in, say, fairness, for instance? You might put forward a negotiated pay settlement to unionised workers that, on paper, is quite generous and thus you might expect them to accept. But what if workers in another industry had been offered less generous terms; might they feel obliged to turn down the offer out of a sense of solidarity and a sense of fairness? This is a nuance that rational classical economics might not traditionally take into account.

What you might say about this

'Why do we believe people will behave rationally?'

'I've modelled product sales based on some pretty hefty assumptions; it's the best I can do, but we need to take them with a pinch of salt – actually predicting how people behave is incredibly complicated.'

'We need to simplify how we explain the pay packages in real and nominal terms.'

Where you can find out more

George Akerlof and Robert J. Shiller, *Animal Spirits: How Human Psychology Drives the Economy, and Why It Matters for Global Capitalism*, Princeton University Press, 2009.

IDEA #33
I can see your halo

He's really great with numbers so I'm sure he'll make a great boss ...

What you need to know

In 1920 the American psychologist Edward Thorndike's study analysing how commanding officers evaluated their soldiers' skills and capabilities across a wide range of metrics was published. Investigating the relationship between the commanding officers' evaluation of the separate characteristics, Thorndike uncovered a puzzlingly high correlation between them. In Thorndike's words, 'it appeared that the estimates of the same man in a number of different traits such as intelligence, industry, technical skill, reliability etc., were very highly correlated and very evenly correlated … it appeared probable that those giving the ratings were unable to analyse out these different aspects of a person's nature and achievement and rate each in independence of the others.' Several more recent studies have shown evidence of this bias in a variety of fields: attractive people are judged to be happier than less attractive people, as well as being perceived to be more intelligent and trustworthy than unattractive individuals (see Idea #4).

Why it matters

Phil Rosenzweig, a business school professor at IMD, popularised the application of the 'halo effect' bias in the corporate world. He has claimed that popular business books such as *In Search of Excellence*, *Built to Last* and *Good to Great* are frequently guilty of this bias; often assuming that a company's high share price must be an indicator of excellent strategic direction or high operating margins can only be the result of visionary leadership. Instead, they mistake correlation with causation or succumb to various other analytical flaws. As Rosenzweig states, '[These books] claim to have identified the drivers of company performance, but they have mainly shown the way that high performers are described.'

A popular variant of the halo effect is the Peter Principle. This is the concept that in most organisations individuals are (with some irony) promoted out of their actual field of competence. This commonly occurs as a result of erroneous logic that, for example, an excellent engineer should surely make a great manager of a team of engineers. The engineer in question may be rewarded for her high performance with promotion to a managerial role, despite the fact that her real strengths may be technical, not managerial.

How this will change the way you work

- *Make a good first impression.* Ensure that your most outward-facing trait – be it your website, the language and tone your customer service team use or your attire – is as polished as possible. The halo effect means individuals are likely to make assumptions about the rest of your business (or your character) based on these first impressions.

- *Capitalise on your halo.* Several companies have successfully branched out into new industries and markets through this method. Apple went from being a niche provider of fancy computers to a firm of mass-market appeal, for instance. Customers bought their new products based on the favourable views they held of their previous products, even if they were completely different in nature. Other firms have been less successful, however – does anyone remember Harley-Davidson perfume?

- *Clarify your assumptions.* To avoid falling into the halo trap, always be explicit about why you believe something. In recruitment processes, for instance, you may be asked to evaluate a candidate against a series of criteria (leadership; interpersonal skills; analytical ability; etc.). Make sure you have clear evidence for your evaluations – it could be that you are basing your evaluation of someone's analytical skills on your (negative or positive) perceptions of their leadership skills. The two need not necessarily be linked.

What you might say about this

'Remember that the skillsets required from a great executive are very different from those needed from a great senior manager.'

'He might be a great analyst, but will that make him a great manager?'

'He's got lucky throughout his career – he had one great success and has lived off it ever since.'

Where you can find out more

'A constant error on psychological ratings', E.L. Thorndike, *Journal of Applied Psychology*, Vol. 4, No. 1, 1920.

Phil Rosenzweig, *The Halo Effect*, The Free Press, 2007.

Laurence J. Peter and Raymond Hull, *The Peter Principle: Why Things Always Go Wrong*, William Morrow & Company, 1969.

IDEA #34
To get to the C-suite, be a generalist

Your odds of getting into the C-suite go up if you've had a generalist background.

What you need to know

How can you get a leadership-level job? Edward Lazear, professor of human resources management and economics at Stanford Graduate School of Business, analysed the career profiles of 5,000 respondents to a 1997 survey of Stanford Business School alumni. Focusing on individuals with at least 15 years of professional experience, Lazear found that individuals who had held two roles or fewer had only a 2 per cent probability of entering the C-suite. By comparison, respondents who had held at least five positions had an 18 per cent chance of reaching senior executive level.

Why it matters

Lazear suggests that the reason for this is because 'the higher you get in an organisation, the more likely you are to encounter problems from a variety of different areas'. In terms of CEOs, he claims that 'a good CEO is someone who's very good, possibly not excellent, but very good, at almost everything'. Having held a variety of jobs and positions inevitably opens you up to new challenges and problems – and this plurality of experience can help you develop the skills required of CEOs. In other words, if you want to get to the top, be a generalist.

How this will change the way you work

- When plotting your career trajectory – if your aim is to get into the C-suite and beyond – think about how you can have a diverse and varied set of career experiences. You don't necessarily need to work at different organisations to have different roles. If you're in a large organisation, see if you can move into different departments to get different experiences. If you're in a smaller firm, you may want to think about secondment opportunities with partner firms.

- You should also consider what type of an organisation you'd like to be a leader of. Lazear's research suggests that the bigger and more diverse the activities of an organisation are, the wider the generalist skills required from their leaders. For example, corporate CEOs have broader backgrounds and skillsets than chairs of academic departments or universities.

What you might say about this

'Are there any secondment opportunities available?'

'I've got a real blind spot in financial accounting. If I want to get to the top I need to sort this out.'

'Everyone on the executive team is a generalist. We need to make sure that between us on the senior team we understand the specialist work going on in the organisation.'

Where you can find out more

'Leadership: A personnel economics approach,' Edward P. Lazear, *National Bureau of Economic Research*, Working Paper Series, April 2010.

IDEA #35
The two yous

Our brain can be thought of as two distinct entities – System 1 (our 'intuitive' self) and System 2 (our 'reasoning' self).

What you need to know

What makes you who you are? Descartes' famous 'cogito ergo sum' ('I think therefore I am') maxim has informed Western concepts of the self for centuries. Through this, the basic principle flows that it is our thoughtful, reflexive, considered selves that dominate our personality. Orthodox economic theory maintains that we are rational beings, governed by reason and logic. However, groundbreaking discoveries in the fields of cognitive psychology, neuroscience and behavioural economics have turned this thinking on its head. According to Daniel Kahneman, instead of thinking of ourselves as thoughtful, rational beings as Cartesian theory would suggest, we should instead consider that there are really two distinct entities that compose our brains. The first is System 1. Automatic, intuitive, and – crucially – the part of our brain that is active most of the time, System 1 is in essence our 'auto-pilot' and default mode of thinking. It is also tremendously prone to error and cognitive biases. The second part of our brain is System 2. The part of our brain which deals with complex, tricky problems, System 2 tires easily. As a result, because

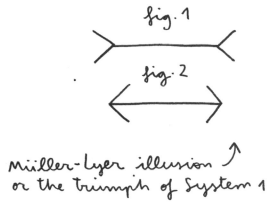

fig. 1

fig. 2

Müller-Lyer illusion ↗
or the triumph of System 1

our brains are inherently lazy, we err towards using System 1 and, as a result, are highly susceptible to making poor decisions.

Why it matters

The fact that most of the time we only engage System 1 has profound implications for how we make decisions in our lives. Because System 1 is often unthinking and uncritical, it tends to make poor choices such as misunderstanding discounts (Idea #8), unfairly discriminating against candidates (Idea #33) or simply make incorrect, snap judgements. In one of the most famous examples of the failures of System 1, consider the Müller-Lyer illusion, illustrated above.

Which line is longer? Intuitively, System 1 will tell you that the top line is longer, but, of course, if you measure them, they are the same size. System 1, with its desire for simplicity and providing answers quickly, has jumped to an incorrect answer. Kahneman proposes a simple yet startling way to show how our brains (and our bodies) cope differently while operating in System 1 and System 2. Next time you are outside walking with a friend and engaging in small-talk, ask them to calculate 34 × 57. They will almost certainly stop in their tracks, their pupils will dilate and, if you were measuring their heartbeat, it would increase too. Ambling along peacefully, System 1 will have been engaged. By asking a difficult and probing question, System 2 will take over and your friend will need to focus attention and effort (previously spread between chit-chat and subconsciously walking) on the question posed.

How this will change the way you work

- Kahneman stresses that overcoming the biases and errors of System 1 is a near-impossible task and – along with his late research partner Amos Tversky – as one of the individuals who have done more than anyone else to highlight the nature of both systems it is wise to take note of this advice.

- However, this does not mean we cannot try to utilise this knowledge. The next time you have to make a difficult decision, or you need to really use all of your brain power, consider if you are engaging System 1 or System 2. If you feel relaxed and comfortable, the reality is that you're probably on little more than mental auto-pilot. In many instances this may be appropriate, but in some circumstances it might be wise to try and snap into System 2 thinking.

- The best way to do this is simply to be aware of your biases – although a couple of tricks may help. For example, try frowning when you're dealing with a difficult problem (Idea #71).

What you might say about this

'Our brains are lazy and try to use up as little energy as possible – this means we often take dangerous mental shortcuts when trying to solve tricky problems.'

'He completely dived in and gave the wrong answer – he hasn't got out of System 1 thinking.'

'Her pupils are dilated – she must be thinking in System 2.'

Where you can find out more

Daniel Kahneman, *Thinking, Fast and Slow*, Penguin: Allen Lane, 2011.

'Overcoming intuition: Metacognitive difficulty activates analytic reasoning', Adam L. Alter, Daniel M. Oppenheimer, Nicholas Epley and Rebecca N. Eyre, *Journal of Experimental Psychology: General*, Vol. 136, No. 4, 2007.

IDEA #36
Work stress? Go for a run

Out of myriad tips and tricks for reducing stress, the simplest might be the best – do some exercise.

What you need to know

Research conducted at the University of Maryland has found that the key to reducing anxiety – which manifests itself in a variety of physiological ways, from muscle tension to feelings of fear and confusion to concentration problems – might just be to undertake some moderate intensity exercise. Using a group of college students as the test base, the study separated the students into two groups: one undertook moderate intensity cycling for 30 minutes; the other rested for 30 minutes. The researchers measured the students' anxiety levels at three points: before the period of exercise or rest; 15 minutes after; and finally after both groups of students had been exposed to a mixture of photographic images designed to arouse a range of positive, distressing and neutral emotions (for instance, the images contained examples ranging from babies and puppies to city landscapes to violent mutilations).

In the measurement based on the students' anxiety levels 15 minutes after their activity or rest, both cohorts experienced similar levels of a reduction in anxiety. However, after exposure to the photographic images, the anxiety levels of the 'rest' group returned to their pre-rest levels, whereas for the 'exercise' group anxiety levels remained as they had been 15 minutes after the cycling. Seemingly, when stress is induced, exercise is more effective than rest in reducing anxiety.

Why it matters

A tremendous amount of research has been undertaken to help companies reduce stress and anxiety levels in the workplace. Everything from developing 'participative leadership cultures' to creating meaningful job roles to adopting daily yoga relaxation sessions has been suggested as the answer to workplace stress. However, while there has rightly been much emphasis on what *employers* can do, there has been less focus on what *employees* can do to help themselves. The University of Maryland's research suggests there may be a simple answer – exercise.

How this will change the way you work

- *Form a habit.* Getting into an exercise routine is never easy, so it would be worth considering some habit-forming tips from Idea #61 to help achieve this. Organisations can facilitate this too. Giving employees protected 'workout time' and providing free or reduced gym memberships can obviously help, but, ultimately, nobody can force you to do exercise, only yourself. When the benefits are so plentiful and obvious, the question should not be 'why should I exercise?', but 'how can I overcome the barriers to doing more exercise?'

What you might say about this

'I've got a big meeting coming up later today. I'm going to go for a run beforehand to help me prepare for it.'

'We can bring in all the health and well-being gurus in the world for corporate advice, but, in the end, we can't force people to do anything.'

'If you need to come in a bit later so you can fit in some gym time this morning that's fine by me – I know how much it can help.'

Where you can find out more

'Effects of emotional exposure on state anxiety after acute exercise', J. Carson Smith, *Medicine and Science in Sports and Exercise*, August 2012.

Pamela Perrewé, Jonathan Halbesleben and Chris Rosen, *Research in Occupational Stress and Well-Being Book Series*, Emerald, 2001–2011.

IDEA #37
The power of peer pressure

The trick to inducing conformity: keeping up with the Joneses.

What you need to know

How do you make people change their behaviour? Peer pressure – a branch of 'nudge theory' advocated by Cass Sunstein – has been consistently demonstrated as a powerful tool for making individuals act differently. Such has been the take-up of the concept that both the British and American governments have begun adopting some of its techniques in a bid to make their citizens more environmentally friendly. This policy development has arisen as a result of a number of high-profile studies highlighting the benefits of the theory. In one paper, two field experiments demonstrated the impact of using signs in hotel guest rooms to encourage residents to reuse their towels. For control and test groups, one sign read 'Show your respect for nature ... reuse your towels', whereas another read 'Join your fellow guests in helping to save the environment ... 75% of our guests are reusing their towels', respectively. In the second instance – where peer pressure was apparent – guests were 25 per cent more likely to reuse their towels. A second field experiment found this positive change in behaviour was even more pronounced when the signs were even more explicitly related to the hotel guests' experience: '75% of the guests who stayed in this room ([room number inserted]) participated in our new resource savings programme by using their towel more than once.' Evidence of positive reactions to such peer pressure has been reported across a variety of energy and health-related settings and countries, including India and China.

Why it matters

Next time you go to the supermarket, consider how easy it is to pick up a shopping bag. Some years ago, these would have been handed out freely, no questions asked. Now, increasing numbers of supermarkets are gently nudging their consumers into more environmentally-friendly actions by making it harder to get bags. Often you have to ask for them – in front of your fellow shoppers, thereby inducing peer pressure to bring your own recyclable bags instead – or even pay for them; as a result, studies have shown supermarket shopping bag use has declined considerably in stores that adopt this approach. The powerful effects of peer pressure can be used in a positive way in a number of environments.

How this will change the way you work

- *Single out the deviants.* If you're trying to get your team or customers to act in a different way, highlighting how their behaviour deviates from that of the majority of their peers provides a powerful incentive for conformity.

- *Beware the so-called 'boomerang effect'.* This is where those already exhibiting 'above average' virtuous behaviour stop their actions because their previous behaviour was based on ignorance of their peer groups. For example, some households may consume little energy compared to their neighbours and in some studies these households – once informed of the fact – actually increased their consumption.

- However, on the whole, the 'boomerang effect' appears to be tempered by two things: first, the positive effects of forcing the worst offenders to improve their behaviours generally offsets any 'boomerang effect'; and, second, messaging can be tailored so that those exhibiting above average virtuous behaviours are not informed of the fact and so are not influenced either positively or negatively by peer pressure.

What you might say about this

'We need you to start completing your timesheets every three minutes from now on. I know it might seem like overkill but 85 per cent of lawyers are already doing this.'

'Write up a digested case study of every project you complete – your predecessor always used to do this very well.'

'Let's use peer pressure to nudge people into action – but we should consider any potential "boomerang effect" first.'

Where you can find out more

'Evidence from two large field experiments that peer comparison feedback can reduce residential energy usage', Ian Ayres, Sophie Raseman and Alice Shih, *The Journal of Law, Economics & Organization*, August 2012.

'A room with a viewpoint: Using social norms to motivate environmental conservation in hotels', Noah J. Goldstein, Robert B. Cialdini and Vladas Griskevicius, *Journal of Consumer Research*, Vol. 35, August 2008.

IDEA #38
The benefits of believing in immanent justice

We're more generous to others when we're hoping for good things to happen that are out of our control.

What you need to know

Across four different experiments researchers from the University of Virginia and Booth School of Business were able to demonstrate how people 'invest in karma' when facing the outcome of important events that are beyond their control. Regardless of any belief or disbelief in the religious or supernatural, individuals consistently demonstrate a willingness to believe that by helping others, somehow the universe will positively conspire to help them in their travails.

In the first experiment, 95 participants were primed to reflect on uncontrollable outcomes they were awaiting – such as medical test results or the verdicts in court cases – compared to another group of participants who were encouraged to think about their daily chores. The group primed to consider events outside of their control were significantly more likely to volunteer greater amounts of their time for charitable causes than those who thought about quotidian routines.

In a second experiment, participants primed to think about uncontrollable outcomes donated more money to charitable causes than those who thought about mundane things such as whether to eat a burger or a pizza. In a third, 'real-world', experiment the researchers surveyed job fair attendees. One group was encouraged to think of employment factors outside of their control (for instance, the state of the economy) while the second group considered factors within their control (such as industry knowledge). The former group pledged more money to charity from a potential $100 lottery prize they were awarded than the latter group.

In the fourth experiment, the causal investigation was reversed, with similar findings. In this experiment, 327 job fair attendees were asked to undertake the same survey as in the third experiment. Half of these respondents were told that by completing the survey they had potentially raised $50 for charity, while the other group were not. The researchers found that it was individuals primed to think that their job prospects were out of their control and they had raised money for charity who were the most positive group when asked about their job prospects – doing good made them feel more optimistic. In the words of the authors, these individuals were demonstrating a belief in 'karmic investment'.

Why it matters

The theory of 'karmic investment' tells us something fascinating about the human psyche: when we're in need of a favour or a lucky break, we're at our most giving and generous and this in turn makes us more optimistic about our prospects. This has important implications for organisational culture. Companies that work in industries under considerable amounts of uncertainty – in recent decades, manufacturing has been a prime example of this – can expect their employees to face great stress in the workplace. Encouraging individuals to offer favours to each other or to donate time to charity might help ease this strain on the individuals and make for a more mutually supportive workplace environment.

How this will change the way you work

- *Charity begins elsewhere.* We all face great strain and stress from time to time, particularly when we feel like things are out of our control. While there is clearly no evidence that helping others or donating money to charity improves the outcomes of our causes of stress, research into 'karmic investment' shows that it can make us feel better about the issues out of our control and more optimistic about the future. Consequently, if you want to feel more positive about something that is concerning you, then consider helping a friend or a charity.

What you might say about this

'When we say "I don't want to tempt fate" we're demonstrating our belief in karma – or what philosophers call "immanent justice".'

'I'm stressed about this issue but I know I can't do anything about it. Helping someone in need will take my mind off things and make me feel better.'

'Helping others isn't just good for them – it's good for us too.'

Where you can find out more

'Investing in karma: When wanting promotes helping', Benjamin A. Converse, Jane L. Risen and Travis J. Carter, *Psychological Science*, July 2012.

IDEA #39
It's lonely at the top

How power leads to scepticism.

What you need to know

In an imaginative study incorporating the musings on love of the German political scientist Hans Morgenthau, researchers from London Business School, Stanford University and Northwestern University have shown the corrosive impact power can have on our ability to trust others. Through five studies covering a variety of workplace and even marital settings, participants were split into high-power and low-power positions. Power was defined in a variety of ways, including job hierarchy (e.g., managers or managees), income disparity or social status. In all instances high-powered individuals, when offered or asked to imagine acts of kindness or generosity towards them from their co-workers, peers or spouse, were less grateful, less likely to reciprocate the generosity and, in the case of married couples, demonstrated less commitment towards their relationship than low-power individuals.

Why it matters

As the authors, paraphrasing Morgenthau, note: 'people seek power because they want to be embraced by others but, once in power, the affection and connections that [they] are offered are tainted by ambiguities surrounding their meaning.' Given how much business depends on trust in relationships, and the knowledge that wide circles of support are needed to succeed in business (see Idea #9), this is worrying news. The fact that power inequalities can compromise trust and engender cynicism needs to be acknowledged by both high-power and lower-power individuals so this unhelpful scepticism can be overcome.

How this will change the way you work

- This research does beg a further question: 'are powerful people right to be more cynical about people trying to use them?' To date, there is little research on the matter, but it is worth bearing in mind when considering the issue. High-powered individuals often have both wealth and reputation to protect, and so excessive caution may not be such a bad thing. But this needs to be carefully moderated – it will be a lonely and unhappy experience at the top for anyone who cannot trust.

What you might say about this

'We need to cut her some slack. I know it feels like she doesn't trust us yet, but even if she doesn't that's understandable – she has a lot to lose.'

'What is driving my cynicism and scepticism? If it's because I think people are trying to take advantage of me, am I justified in thinking this?'

'Every CEO needs somebody they can really trust and confide in.'

Where you can find out more

'How power corrupts relationships: Cynical attributions for others' generous acts', M. Ena Inesi, Deborah H. Gruenfeld and Adam D. Galinsky, *Journal of Experimental Social Psychology*, Vol. 48, No. 4, 2012.

IDEA #40
It's not what you said, it's how you said it

What our use of function words says about us.

What you need to know

Function words – which include articles (*a, the*), pronouns (*you, they*), prepositions (*to, for*), and auxiliary verbs (*is, have*) – account for only around 0.5 per cent of the average speaker's vocabulary, yet make up over half of all words actually spoken. According to James Pennebaker, a social psychologist from the University of Texas, it's these few words that can provide the biggest insight into someone's character – such as how confident they are or the truthfulness of what they are saying. Over the past 20 years Pennebaker has analysed – with the help of a computer model – more than 400,000 texts covering personal conversations, love letters, poems, tweets, blogs and even the diaries of victims of traumatic experiences. In so doing, Pennebaker has been able to pinpoint some tell-tale facts that our use of diction betrays about us.

Why it matters

Pennebaker's research suggests two fascinating clues to a person's state of mind: the first is to do with lying. Here, his studies have uncovered that when individuals frequently use pronouns such as 'we', or use simple, definitive statements (such as 'It's *clear* that *we* have *never* ...'), this may often be an indication of evasion. Second, Pennebaker suggests that the use of 'I' (such as in 'I think ...') is important, but in unexpected ways. We often equate the sustained use of the pronoun 'I' with arrogance – as was the case in many political commentators' analyses of President Obama's address to the nation following the killing of Osama bin Laden. In actual fact, Pennebaker claims that frequent use of 'I' is more often an indicator of a lack of confidence. Consider the following statements you might utter to one of your team members: 'I think your analysis might contain some errors' or 'There are errors here.' The statements are largely saying the same thing, but the subtext is clear: the former hints to some insecurity and uncertainty, whereas the latter implies confidence and definitiveness.

How this will change the way you work

- Confidence, for any manger and leader, is vital. Often expected to be responsible for projects or budgets that they have little direct oversight or engagement with, a game is occasionally played with shareholders or colleagues where managers and leaders need to give confidence that they have complete mastery of the detail, even if the opposite is sometimes true. So how can Pennebaker's work help here? The key is in analysing your own language and then eliminating any redundant 'I's. Double-check your emails before hitting send, listen to what you say as you speak or even go so far as to record yourself delivering a speech. As you do so, check how often you use terms such as 'I think' or 'I feel'.

- As a benchmark, a typical 'over-user' of 'I' will use the term in around 6.5 per cent of all words spoken in a passage; compared to about 4 per cent of the time for a 'regular' user of 'I'. Where do you fit on this scale? If you're an 'over-user', why is this so and what can you do about it?

What you might say about this

'It's not a case of "*I think* this or that" – this is simply true.'

'Let me give you some feedback: you need to watch your use of prepositions. Your over-use of "I" is making you sound unsure.'

'Analyse your emails carefully before sending them – they might say more than you think.'

Where you can find out more

James W. Pennebaker, *The Secret Life of Pronouns: What Our Words Say About Us*, Bloomsbury Publishing, 2011.

'Your use of pronouns reveals your personality', James W. Pennebaker, *Harvard Business Review*, December 2011.

IDEA #41
Find out when you're in the zone

We flit between high and low periods of productivity.

What you need to know

Analysing data from more than 12 studies tracing the lives of individuals over 50 years, Finnish researchers uncovered the worrying observation that workers who consistently spend long hours in the office (defined as more than eight hours a day) have a 40 per cent increased risk of coronary heart disease. Bearing this in mind, the imperative to keep working hours manageable is stronger than ever – but this means our workload will necessarily have to reduce. As a result, the next question is 'how can we maximise our productivity during the hours that we do work?'

Why it matters

A growing body of research has suggested that most adults are at their peak of productivity in the late morning, with attention and focus decreasing from midday to 4 p.m. Sleepiness is at its most pronounced after meals. Intriguingly, another study found that student participants were actually at their most creative at the times they perceived themselves to be at their least productive – so while our most productive hours (known as the peak of our circadian rhythm) might be good for getting stuff done, they may be less good for getting our creative juices flowing. The researchers hypothesised that this might be because when we are least alert we are able to engage the more novel and less exercised parts of our brain that inspire creative thought.

How this will change the way you work

- Work out when your productivity peak is. To do this, keep a log of the actions you have completed over the course of a week, split by day of the week and hour of day. When looking back at your week, focus in on the hours where you believe you have completed either the most complex or greatest volume of tasks. From this, you should be able to calculate your peak productivity time.

- Match demand to the peak. In the future, plan your day so as far as possible when you need to crack on with a large number of actions you do this at your peak productivity time. By contrast, use the hours that you calculate to be your lowest productivity times to undertake work that requires creative thought.

What you might say about this

'I'm a morning person – I need to protect this time so I can use it to get the most tasks done.'

'Mid-afternoon is usually a slow period for most people – we should avoid booking in any important meetings then.'

'I need to work out when I'm at the peak of my circadian rhythm.'

Where you can find out more

'Time of day effects on problem-solving: When the non-optimal is optimal', Mareike B. Wieth and Rose T. Zacks, *Thinking & Reasoning*, Vol. 17, No. 4, 2011.

'Long working hours and coronary heart disease: A systematic review and meta-analysis', Marianna Virtanen, Katriina Heikkilä, Markus Jokela, Jane E. Ferrie, G. David Batty, Jussi Vahtera and Mika Kivimäki, *American Journal of Epidemiology*, Vol. 176, No. 10, 2012.

'Chronotype and time-of-day influences on the alerting, orienting, and executive components of attention', Robert L. Matchock and J. Toby Mordkoff, *Experimental Brain Research*, Vol. 192, No. 2, 2012.

IDEA #42
To really improve, just do it

Fortunes are spent each year on business training courses and books – but if you really want to improve, nothing beats doing something over and over again.

What you need to know

Have you ever heard a variant of the following: 'I want to be treated at the best hospital, so I'm going to a small hospital with specialised, dedicated care'? While a quiet, local hospital that only handles a low number of patients might seem like the best place for clinical care, there is incontrovertible evidence that in medicine – as in most professions – volume is everything. In a 2008 study of treatment by physicians for more than 40,000 HIV sufferers, the only variable explaining patient mortality to a statistically significant level was patient volume. In other words, the greater the numbers of patients that doctors see, the better the outcomes they deliver.

Malcolm Gladwell, in his bestselling book *Outliers: The Story of Success*, studied a range of high-profile success stories from Bill Gates to The Beatles and popularised the idea of the '10,000 hour rule' – that the key to expertise and success in any field is to practise specific and repeatable tasks (related to the desired area of success) for 10,000 hours. While the exact number may not be conclusively proven, the point nonetheless remains – practice, much more than study, really does make perfect.

Why it matters

This has major implications for personal development. Companies spend billions each year sending their employees on expensive training courses, often with very little demonstrable return on investment. While there are undoubtedly benefits from training courses such as increased employee satisfaction, if we recognise that the primary purpose of such training is to improve participant capability, yet know there to be more effective ways of doing this, why do we continue to spend so much on training? Diligent practice combined with on-the-job learning, unfashionable though it may sound, is by far the most evidence-based and reliable way to really improve skills.

How this will change the way you work

- If you have a particular skill or competency you want to develop (e.g., mastering writing computer code), create a working environment in which you will necessarily have to repeat the skill continuously. If this isn't possible, set up regular time slots in your day-to-day life to practise the competency outside of working hours – calendars and email reminders can be helpful to get you into the rhythm of doing this.

- Be diligent. 10,000 hours is effectively 20 hours a week, every week for ten years. Very few people will ever hit this figure for a specific, honed, skill, but it's still important to set challenging goals for dedicated practice time – if you don't set aside a given number of hours each week for practice, you almost certainly won't achieve it.

- Quantify your improvements. As discussed in Idea #44, if you can't measure your improvements how will you know if you've succeeded? Set yourself two types of goals: one input based (i.e., number of hours of practice or assignments undertaken); and one output based (i.e., measurable improvement in performance or qualification achieved).

What you might say about this

'To become really excellent at something requires a long-term investment of time and effort – you can't just learn it overnight in a textbook.'

'This person doesn't have much experience doing this kind of work. I know they're smart, but isn't it a bit of a risk employing them to do this?'

'Real improvements come from experience, so let's cut the training and development budget and use the money on something people will value more.'

Where you can find out more

'Practice makes perfect: A volume–outcome study of hospital patients with HIV disease', F. Hellinger, *Journal of Acquired Immune Deficiency Syndromes*, February 2008.

Malcolm Gladwell, *Outliers: The Story of Success*, Penguin: Allen Lane, 2008.

'Towards an understanding of learning by doing: Evidence from an automobile assembly plant', Steve D. Levitt, John A. List and Chad Syverson, *National Bureau of Economic Research*, Working Paper, April 2012.

IDEA #43
To decide alone is to make a bad decision

The best decision-makers are those who actively canvass and act upon a diverse array of opinions and views.

What you need to know

In 1906, the 84-year-old great Victorian statistician Sir Francis Galton visited the annual West of England Fat Stock and Poultry Exhibition. At the exhibition, Galton came across an ox weight-judging competition. Paying sixpence eight each, 800 people entered the competition, many of whom Galton observed as being 'non-experts'. Galton collected all the responses from the organisers and ran some statistical tests. Taking the median of all the estimates, the crowd guessed the weight of the ox to be 1,197 pounds. The actual weight turned out to be 1,198 pounds. The wisdom of the exhibition crowd was correct to within 1 per cent. As Galton wrote in the summary of his experiment in the scientific journal *Nature*, 'The result seems more creditable to the trustworthiness of a democratic judgement than might have been expected.'

Why it matters

The 'cult of the CEO' has led to an unhealthy – and dangerous – expectation that corporate wisdom rests in the minds of a few exulted organisation leaders. The legal scholar Cass Sunstein argues that major recent flawed governmental and corporate sector decisions, such as the justification for the Iraq War, Enron accounting cover-ups and the Columbia space shuttle disaster can be explained by 'information cocoons', where leaders and key decision-making groups failed to take account of the wide and diverse array of opinions and information available to them. With technology making it easier to engage large numbers of stakeholders in decisions, it is simpler than ever before to overcome these 'groupthink' failures. However, even when large groups of individuals do form to make decisions there are still clearly instances of poor 'crowd wisdom' – stock market bubbles, for instance. To avoid these forms of 'rational bubbles', all opinions canvassed in group decisions need to be *independently formed*. Writers such as James Surowiecki have stressed that the root cause of most instances of failure of the 'wisdom of crowds' lies in a system failure. This is where individuals are too conscious of the opinions of others and thus neglect any private information they may possess and instead conform to 'groupthink'.

How this will change the way you work

- *Always ask others for input on decisions – especially difficult ones.* The information management company EMC Corporation, when seeking advice on where to find organisational efficiencies, asked its workforce where to cut costs. Not only were inefficiencies found that the senior management were previously unaware of but also, when they were acted upon, the moves possessed greater legitimacy from the workforce as they had been involved in the process.

- *Avoid 'information cascades'.* This is where individuals observe the actions of others (usually senior to them) and then act upon them, even if they are contrary to their own beliefs or private information. In the workplace, encourage an inquisitive environment – it is good for individuals to question why they are doing things. Just because 'someone else is doing it too' isn't a good enough reason.

- *Celebrate information.* Use social media to encourage information-sharing within your organisation. Wikis, forums and surveys are simple ways organisations can share and gain insights and knowledge from a diverse array of sources. The more diverse your information inputs, the better your decision-making outputs.

What you might say about this

'Leadership doesn't mean only one person can make decisions.'

'Let's ask what our staff and customers actually want.'

'Are we basing our decision on what we've historically done? Maybe we need a fresh view.'

Where you can find out more

James Surowiecki, *The Wisdom of Crowds: Why the Many Are Smarter Than The Few*, Abacus, 2004.

Cass R. Sunstein, *Infotopia: How Many Minds Produce Knowledge*, Oxford University Press, 2006.

'Vox populi', Francis Galton, *Nature*, Vol. 75, 1907.

IDEA #44
If you can't measure it, it's likely to be rubbish

SELECTION PROCESS

Statistical or mechanical predictions trump clinical or intuitive ones.

What you need to know

In 1954 the psychologist Paul Meehl published a groundbreaking book that transformed our understanding of the accuracy and nature of predictions and assessments. Meehl analysed the findings of 20 studies that compared the accuracy of clinical predictions (based on a subjective assessment of a topic, usually incorporating a wide variety of inputs – for instance, judging an essay-writing competition is largely a 'subjective assessment') against statistical predictions (formed from ratings ascribed to a small number of criteria – for instance, multiple choice answer examination is an 'objective assessment'). Across studies covering high-school grade achievement in students, parole violation and even pilot training, Meehl found a shocking degree of consensus in the conclusion that statistical predictions overwhelmingly trumped clinical ones in their ability to forecast the future performance of individuals.

Why it matters

The behavioural economist Daniel Kahneman was greatly influenced by Meehl's work. Recounting one of his first tasks in the Israeli Defence Force, Kahneman set up an army interview system that superseded the previous evaluation process, whereby candidates undertook interviews of up to 20 minutes and the interviewer was encouraged to cover a range of topics and form a 'general impression' of the interviewee. In its place, Kahneman installed an interview evaluation scoring process, covering six topics (for factors such as 'sociability' and 'masculine pride'), which interviewers would then score on a scale of 1 to 5. Accepted soldiers' performance evaluations in subsequent months were better following the introduction of statistical prediction in the interview process. As Kahneman surmised, 'the sum of our six ratings predicted soldiers' performance much more accurately than the global evaluations of the previous interviewing method.' Although, as he notes, this remained 'far from perfect', as predictions are a notoriously tricky undertaking, quantification and the use of statistics helped upgrade the evaluation process from being 'completely useless' to 'moderately useful'.

How this will change the way you work

- The great Victorian mathematical physicist Lord Kelvin famously said, 'If you cannot measure it, you cannot improve it.' Yet we continue to make decisions in business based on gut instinct or highly subjective evaluations. While there is a danger in always trying to measure everything – both in that it is time-consuming and sometimes a bad measurement can be worse than no measurement – without hard quantification it is near-impossible to either demonstrate progress or, worse, make non-biased decisions.

- Quantifying decisions helps us confront and make transparent our tendency to make poor decisions on factors that don't matter. The next time you have a difficult strategic assessment to make, create a scoring criteria evaluation beforehand, then base your decision on the scoring of your criteria.

- Don't believe that it's impossible to quantify everything – even something as ethereal as 'happiness' is now measured and tracked by several governments. Using surveys that invite participants to quantitatively score metrics (on a scale of 1 to 5, for instance) on hard to pin down topics can help give you a solid figure to base your judgements on.

What you might say about this

'In isolation, statistical predictions are much better than clinical predictions, but the trick is in marrying the two together.'

'How can we use data to improve our decision-making?'

'Choose your criteria for evaluation carefully – these will have a big impact on how you quantify something.'

Where you can find out more

Paul Everett Meehl, *Clinical Versus Statistical Prediction: A Theoretical Analysis and a Review of the Evidence*, University of Minnesota Press, 1954.

Daniel Kahneman, *Thinking, Fast and Slow*, Penguin: Allen Lane, 2011.

IDEA #45
That's my (one) goal

Setting yourself multiple goals can reduce your chances of meeting any of them.

What you need to know

Any self-respecting coach will tell you that to achieve fulfilment you need to work out what you want, set goals that represent your wants, work out a plan to meet your goals, then successfully follow your plan. Easy. However, research from Amy Dalton and Stephen Spiller (of Hong Kong University and UCLA, respectively) suggests that – for consumers at least – planning for more than one goal actually reduces one's ability to achieve them. Using a combination of field and laboratory experiments, the study discovered that where participants had one particular task they needed to accomplish (for example, 'eat a salad with low-fat dressing at lunch tomorrow in the cafeteria') planning for this led to both an increase in the participant commitment to doing so and to the likelihood of them completing the task. By contrast, when participants had multiple tasks and planned for each of them, this actually reduced commitment and achievement.

Why it matters

The researchers hypothesise that planning, rather than helping to overcome likely obstacles to achievement, actually focuses the mind on all the obstacles and challenges that are in the way of success. As a result, too much planning can lead to a mental overload of difficulties ahead. Intriguingly, the experiments found that this fear of overload abated when participants compared their to-do lists with those of others and as a consequence determined, in reality, their action list was more manageable than they initially thought. How we assess the difficulty of our own to-do lists is determined by how view the action lists of others.

How this will change the way you work

- Hone your key goals down to a very small number. It might help to do this by having a 'meta-goal' (i.e., get healthy) and then have sub-actions to achieve this (i.e., eat a low-fat salad today; go for a run tonight).

- Keep detailed planning to a minimum – only plan for what really matters. Too much planning can result in the well-known phrase 'analysis paralysis' – if you overthink something you can scare yourself into inaction.

- If you are feeling swamped with actions, compare your to-do list with a colleague's or friend's. Realising that others also have lots on their plate might help you reappraise your own challenges in a more positive light.

What you might say about this

'I've got a million and one things to do, but actually, only three of them really matter right now.'

'I know I've got it tough, but, to be honest, we all do.'

'I find action lists and plans can be a bit distracting. As long as we make sure we do what we say we'll do, we don't need a huge project plan for every minute task.'

Where you can find out more

'Too much of a good thing: The benefits of implementation intentions depend on the number of goals', Amy N. Dalton and Stephen A. Spiller, *Journal of Consumer Research*, Vol. 39, No. 3, 2012.

IDEA #46
Don't pretend you can always control your emotions

It's not always possible to emotionally disengage from difficult tasks such as lay-offs – the best you can do is manage how you deal with them.

What you need to know

Lay-offs, disciplinary matters, negative performance reviews and the like are part and parcel of the corporate world. Businesses would not be able to operate without these 'necessary evils' and many would claim that they are, in fact, ultimately beneficial – a bloated organisation can only prosper if it is 'trimmed' and redundancies made.

Joshua Margolis and Andrew Molinsky, from the universities of Harvard and Brandeis, respectively, wanted to explore what the emotional impact of such 'necessary evils' is on those who deliver them. Analysing the thoughts and behaviours of more than 110 harbingers of bad news – comprising managers, medics, police officers and counsellors – they found that:

- more than half of all participants became emotionally engaged in difficult tasks such as lay-offs, painful medical procedures, repossessions, expulsions, etc.;

- necessary evils were performed with sensitivity (such as taking actions to minimise the embarrassment of an individual receiving a disciplinary rebuke) in 72 per cent of cases analysed;

- in 55 per cent of all incidents tracked, individuals tailored their approaches to delivering the difficult news away from recommended standard operating procedures.

Why it matters

In a well-cited 1982 article in the *Journal of Health and Social Behavior* the tale was recounted of a nurse who, when confronted with the unenviable task of informing patients and relatives of terminal illnesses, suggested that in order to deliver compassionate care she needed to allow herself to engage with her emotional sadness at the situation. In business, the reverse is often suggested. Managers who are responsible for frequently delivering news of redundancies are encouraged to 'emotionally disengage' from their difficult tasks, as it will prove too emotionally draining. However Margolis and Molinsky's research suggests that such disengagement is an illusion; neither practical nor particularly desirable – turning on its head much management orthodoxy.

How this will change the way you work

- *Support the deliverers of 'necessary evils'.* If up to half the time seasoned individuals, experienced in delivering bad news, engage with the issue at hand emotionally, one can only imagine the psychological toll this must take. Ensure that you – and those around you – are aware of this and support these individuals as appropriate.

- *Embrace emotionality.* If you are intending to deliver bad news soon work through different scenarios with a trusted colleague or friend where you deliver the bad news in different ways.

- *Don't be afraid to deviate from the script.* Most organisations that specialise in meting out 'necessary evils' ensure that staff have a carefully prepared script to help them. These can be useful in facilitating emotional disengagement, but need to be flexible to take account of the fact that, in some instances, no matter all the best-laid plans, it will not be possible to put feelings to one side.

What you might say about this

'I bet he's not as hard-nosed as he seems. Delivering bad news all the time must take its toll on him.'

'She's had a hard time lately with the number or redundancies in her team. We should make sure we recognise this somehow.'

'We're not robots. You can't just shut off your emotions whenever you want to.'

Where you can find out more

'Death telling: Managing the delivery of bad news', R.E. Clark and E.E. LaBeff, *Journal of Health and Social Behavior*, Vol. 23, No. 4, 1982.

'Navigating the bind of necessary evils: Psychological engagement and the production of interpersonally sensitive behaviour', Joshua D. Margolis and Andrew Molinsky, *Academy of Management Journal*, Vol. 51, No. 5, 2008.

IDEA #47
Boost creativity by making the workplace an emotional roller coaster

Looking to increase creativity? Capitalise on your employees' mood swings.

What you need to know

Jennifer George and Jing Zhou of Rice University wanted to understand what got the creative juices going at a large oilfield services company. Among their sample of more than 160 individuals with educational qualifications ranging from high school diplomas to doctorates, George and Zhou tested for three factors: the state of mind of employees (both positive and negative); how employees evaluated their supervisors (across the three dimensions of fairness, feedback and trustworthiness); and how creative supervisors felt their employees were. Surprisingly, the researchers found that high levels of creativity were most likely to occur when employees had recently experienced both highly positive moods and highly negative moods and felt strong support from their supervisors; the switch between positive and negative moods (or vice versa), supplemented by strong line manager support, appeared to be key to unlocking creativity.

Why it matters

Most research into creativity strongly links it to either positive moods (on the basis that when individuals are relaxed or happy they are most likely to think laterally) or negative moods (on the reasoning that when people are in a negative state of mind they are most likely to spot problems and then find out how to solve them). Prior to the research from Rice University there was no reconciliation of this seemingly contradictory evidence. Thanks to George and Zhou's study, we can hypothesise that, in isolation, positive or negative moods are not enough. It is the oscillation between the two – while supported by a compassionate and competent manager – that really engenders creativity.

How this will change the way you work

In practice, of course, this does not mean that managers should actively seek to induce volatile emotional environments in the workplace, but it does suggest two things:

- There needs to be a greater appreciation of the potential positive benefits that negative emotions can bring to the workplace. If somebody is having a tough time, this can be reframed as an opportunity to solve a problem rather than an invitation to wallow in it.

- Managers need to be sensitively attuned to the moods of those whom they manage and, at all times, they need to be supportive and caring – beyond being just good management practice, it might help spur on a 'eureka' moment.

What you might say about this

'How can you turn this challenge into an opportunity?'

'It's the individuals who emotionally yo-yo a bit who are potentially our greatest creative asset.'

'I know things have been a bit up and down at the moment, but how can I best support you as your manager?'

Where you can find out more

'Dual tuning in a supportive context: Joint contributions of positive mood, negative mood, and supervisory behaviors to employee creativity', Jennifer M. George and Jing Zhou, *Academy of Management Journal*, Vol. 50, No. 3, 2007.

IDEA #48
Escaping the cycle of responsiveness

The benefits of turning off your email and mobile phone.

What you need to know

Turn off my smartphone? Don't be ridiculous! How could my team cope without being able to contact me 24/7? How can I not be at my client's beck and call? How will I be able to show what a hard worker I am by not sending emails at 2 a.m.?!

Facing similar concerns, Leslie Perlow – Konosuke Matsushita professor of leadership at Harvard Business School – tested her hypothesis that switching off smartphones (at selected times) makes for happier and more productive teams at one of the archetypal hard-working service organisations: the Boston Consulting Group. Starting as an experiment with a six-person BCG team, Perlow managed to spread successfully the gospel of sleeping *without* your smartphone across 900 BCG teams spanning five continents. Perlow encouraged teams to agree on setting 'predictable time off' (or 'PTO'), such as a night a week when workers down tools at a respectable time, with their time off protected – with no panic emails or calls allowed to reach them from colleagues, clients or leaders.

Despite facing some scepticism – and not to say unwillingness, as some consultants actually enjoy all-hours working patterns – the results from Perlow's experiments at BCG were quite incredible. Comparing surveys of consultants engaged in PTO experiments against those who were not, 72 per cent (against 49 per cent not in PTOs) were satisfied with their job; 54 per cent (against 38 per cent in PTOs) were content with their work–life balance; and, quite astonishingly, PTO teams also felt themselves to be more collaborative (91 per cent agreed versus 76 per cent) more efficient (65 per cent agreed versus 42 per cent) and more effective (74 per cent agreed versus 51 per cent). The list of happy findings continued, with PTO team members also more likely to see a long-term future at BCG and believe they were providing 'significant value to their clients' than non-PTO members.

Why it matters

Perlow began her research on the back of a survey of more than 1,600 workers who, in all instances, had a highly favoured inclination to check emails first thing in the morning, last thing at night, on weekends and even on holidays. Employees, it seems, are almost always 'on' and available, waiting for the next ping of an incoming email. Besides Perlow's findings, there is a noticeable trend towards greater connectivity, longer working hours and a much stronger expectation that workers are available long after leaving the office. This does not seem to have made for happier workers (and the jury is out as to whether it has made for more productive ones either). Perlow's counter-intuitive, yet reassuring, work suggests that we can be happier – without compromising productivity – by switching off our smartphones every once in a while.

How this will change the way you work

- As part of any team kick-off session it should be the role of the team leader to lay down some ground rules for realistic connectivity expectations. Agreeing 'predictable time off' dates is relatively easy: in theory these should be weekends and beyond absurdly late times in the evening for most service industries. The trick is in enforcing these.

- Team leaders should be highly sensitive to the fact that going 'offline' doesn't make one lazy or lacking in drive – it's actually a very sensible and effective way to keep team morale and satisfaction up.

- Organisation leaders should role model this good practice from the top. It's OK to turn off your email every once in a while.

What you might say about this

'We never work on weekends. If I find teams working on Saturdays or Sundays I won't blame the worker, I'll blame the team leader – it's their responsibility to stop this from happening.'

'Let's set some ground rules and expectations for when people can be contacted and ensure everyone in the company is aware of them.'

'Having PTO doesn't mean you can abnegate responsibility for your work. I expect you to always leave things in such a way that before you go offline there's a suitable person to fill in for you if need be.'

Where you can find out more

Leslie A. Perlow, *Sleeping with Your Smartphone: How to Break the 24/7 Habit and Change the Way You Work*, Harvard Business Review Press, 2012.

IDEA #49
Want to do the right thing? Wait a moment ...

Delayed decision-making leads to better and more ethical decisions.

What you need to know

In writing *Wait: The Art and Science of Delay*, Frank Partnoy – a former Morgan Stanley banker turned professor at the University of San Diego – wanted to understand the reasons behind the financial turmoil of 2008. Surveying the academic literature on the impact of timing in decision-making from the fields of finance, economics and psychology, Partnoy concluded that the pace of life of modern capitalism leads to snap decisions being made – to the detriment of achieving the best possible outcomes. Citing a range of examples, from surgeons reducing mortality rates by delaying their actions through using checklists to how the best tennis players delay their shots by fractions of a second in order to gather and assess more information about the flight of the ball and the position of their opponents, Partnoy's message is clear: time spent waiting to make a decision is not time wasted.

Why it matters

The gospel of increasing productivity seems to rule the workplace. There are few industries where increasing output within an allotted time is not a prized aim: doctors must attend to more patients; pilots fly more planes; journalists write more copy. What if this desire to do more with less time actually leads to worse outcomes?

Research featured in the *Academy of Management Journal* in early 2012 led to some surprising supporting evidence for Partnoy's thesis. Investigating 'right–wrong' choices (epitomised by experiments where the option of lying leads to financial gain for participants), the researchers found that those taking part in the experiments were five times more likely to make an ethical choice (in this instance, not lie) if they were given more time to think about the choice than if they were coerced into making an immediate decision.

How this will change the way you work

- *Take a break before that big decision.* Partnoy has suggested that organisations which place a premium on fast-paced decisions – financial institutions being the exemplar – should implement processes that lead to 'cooling-down' periods for reflections. As one of the authors of the report in the *Academy of Management Journal*, J. Keith Murnighan, opined, 'Executives know what types of decisions raise moral flags in their companies. If people make these decisions electronically, their computers might be programmed to require contemplation time before decisions are finalised – and [they could] even fill this time with reminders of the firm's ethical values.'

What you might say about this

'I'll sleep on it.'

'We measure productivity in terms of quantity of output, but do we also meaningfully measure it in terms of quality of outcome?'

'What's the rush?'

Where you can find out more

'Contemplation and conversation: Subtle influence on moral decision making', Brian C. Gunia, Long Wang, Li Huang, Jiunwen Wang and J. Keith Murnighan, *Academy of Management Journal*, Vol. 55, No. 1, 2012.

Frank Partnoy, *Wait: The Art and Science of Delay*, Public Affairs, 2012.

IDEA #50
Online procrastination – the key to higher productivity

Web surfing can serve as a powerful mental restorative function and lead to increased productivity in workers ... so long as they don't check their emails.

What you need to know

In 2011 Vivien K.G. Lim and Don J.Q. Chen of the National University of Singapore undertook a study of 96 undergraduate management students to assess the impact of web surfing on their productivity. Initially, 96 students spent 20 minutes highlighting all the letter 'e's that they could spot in a document. The students were then grouped into three sets. The first group (control group) spent ten minutes continuing with a similarly tedious task; the second group were allowed a ten-minute break to do anything of their choosing – except go online (rest group); and the third group were allowed to do whatever they liked online for ten minutes (web surfer group). Then, all three groups spent the next ten minutes highlighting letters again.

The results were surprising. In the final bout of letter highlighting, the web surfers were more productive (i.e., highlighted more letters correctly) than the control group and 16 per cent more productive than the rest group. The web surfers also reported higher levels of engagement and lower levels of both mental fatigue and boredom than the other two groups.

Why it matters

The Internet plays a huge role in the way the business world works. Increasingly, some organisations – concerned with improving productivity and efficiency – have sought to ban or restrict personal Internet use at work. Lim and Chen's research brings into question the effectiveness of such interdictions. However, the researchers have emphasised in previous studies that there is an important cognitive distinction between online surfing and checking emails. In the case of the former, the experience is restorative and pleasurable – you can, in essence 'zone out' while surfing the web. However, checking emails is much more mentally demanding and draining and therefore less restful.

How this will change the way you work

- *Strike a balance.* If your organisation has a draconian 'no personal Internet usage' policy you should certainly reconsider this. However, you can go too far in the opposite direction – you may want to put a time limit on how long people can use the Internet for non-work-related functions. Software packages exist that allow access to normally restricted websites (i.e., non-work-related) to be lifted for a certain amount of time; this could help give people the break and productivity boost they need without allowing people to spend too much time cyberloafing or checking emails.

- *Aim for reasonableness.* In the words of Chen, 'acceptable Internet use policy does not mean a total ban of non-work-related usage of the Internet; it should aim to work out a reasonable balance between some personal web usage and work. More resources should be devoted to curbing detrimental cyberloafing such as emailing while some web browsing should be allowed as a coping strategy against work stress.'

What you might say about this

'Let's take a more relaxed stance on our Internet usage policy.'

'We've been working hard – everyone take a ten-minute break. Feel free to get online and do whatever you need to do.'

'I don't really care what you do so long as you get the job done.'

Where you can find out more

'Impact of cyberloafing on psychological engagement', V.K.G. Lim and D.J.Q. Chen, *Academy of Management Annual Meeting*, 2011.

'Cyberloafing at the workplace: Gain or drain on work?', V.K.G. Lim and D.J.Q. Chen, *Behaviour& Information Technology*, Vol. 31, No. 4, 2012.

IDEA #51
When customers will put up with rude service

In phone-based service industries, customers may be willing to sacrifice politeness for getting what they want.

What you need to know

Lorna Doucet analysed 142 customer service calls at a large north-eastern US retail bank to understand the impact of the rudeness of call representatives on how customers perceive the service quality they receive. With a team of researchers both listening in to calls, and following up with the customers in a survey 48 hours later, Doucet made some surprising discoveries:

- Call representatives' rudeness was generally ignored by customers, as long as the customers got the outcome (e.g., information or action from the representative) they desired. Rudeness had no demonstrable impact on how customers rated the service quality when surveyed by Doucet and her researchers.

- If customers did not receive the outcome they were looking for, however, the behaviour and tone of representatives did seem to have an impact on service evaluation. Any perception of rudeness from the representatives had a negative impact on how customers evaluated the call. By contrast, if representatives couldn't help but were especially polite or apologetic, customers reacted positively and tended to rate service quality highly.

- Call representatives who sounded hostile or rude on the phone tended to have had a longer period of tenure compared with representatives with a less hostile telephone manner. Lorna Doucet suggested this may be a consequence of the stress of call centres and the subsequent burnout that may occur in representatives.

Why it matters

As actual face-to-face interactions with customers decrease for many service providers, the telephone call centre is fast becoming one of the few points of contact between a customer and company. Consequently, companies should devote considerable efforts to understanding what customers really want when they call for help. Doucet's research uncovered that not only do some customers value politeness differently but also in many instances it is very much a secondary concern when it comes to actually having their needs met. Much training for call centre representatives is focused on providing 'good customer service' and being polite to callers, but in reality, this matters much less than being effective. Perhaps training should focus much more on competency rather than politeness.

How this will change the way you work

Doucet suggests in her research three ways that these findings can help managers be more targeted and effective in what they do:

- *Improve the weakest first.* Managers might only need to focus on customer handling training when call representatives are technically poor. In other words, if call representatives are unable to help customers, then it is especially important that they are polite and apologetic.

- *Segment customers by needs.* Doucet notes that 'customers differ in the level of importance they place on service interactions'. By intelligently segmenting customers into those who value high-quality service interactions (i.e., from particularly polite call representatives) and customers who prefer speed and efficiency, call centres might be able to route customers to the most appropriate call representative for them.

- *Refresh employee skills.* The finding that hostility towards customers is most pronounced in call representatives with long tenure suggests that an element of retraining or focused management oversight is necessary for those call handlers who have been around in the organisation for a while.

What you might say about this

'After two years here everyone gets a refresher training session on customer call handling.'

'We can be the kindest and most polite people on the phone, but we mustn't lose sight of the fact we're ultimately meant to help people.'

'If you can't actually help the customer then the least you can do is be friendly and apologetic.'

Where you can find out more

'Service provider hostility and service quality', Lorna Doucet, *Academy of Management Journal*, Vol. 47, No. 5, 2004.

IDEA #52
It's easier to be forgiven than to ask for permission

Individuals judge future potential ethical transgressions (that haven't occurred yet) worse than misdeeds already committed.

What you need to know

Eugene Caruso, an associate professor of behavioural science at the Booth School of Business, University of Chicago, analysed seven different studies where participants judged a potential ethical transgression to be both more unfair and prompt worse negative emotions if they believed the transgression was still to take place than if it had already. In one study, 1,600 individuals at Harvard University were confronted with the following issue. A well-known soft drinks manufacturer was developing a vending machine (located in a far-away state) where the prices of its beverages would positively correlate with the temperature outside. For instance, a drink would cost $1.00 on a cool day and $3.50 on a hot day. Roughly half of the group of 1,600 were told this machine *had already been installed* the previous month (Group A); the others were told the machine *would be installed* the following month (Group B). To a statistically significant extent, the group that believed the prices were going to be changed according to the weather in the future (Group B) felt this was more unfair and prompted more negative emotions than those who believed prices had already been manipulated previously (Group A).

Why it matters

Research by Daniel Kahneman and others has already shown that flexing the price of goods according to Mother Nature is looked upon poorly by consumers. However Caruso's research suggests that *when* the controversial action takes places matters, too. This has serious ethical, legal and commercial repercussions. For instance, does this mean that punishments meted out to potential fraudsters are disproportionately harsher than actual ones? In the workplace, how does this impact on your consistency as an employer? Do you come down more strongly on individuals who have been caught planning a misdemeanour than on those who have already committed one?

How this will change the way you work

- *Play to the future.* The finding that emotions are heightened when considering activities in the future than those in the past suggests that 'playing to the future' may be a powerful way to influence individuals. For instance, when trying to explain a new way of working to individuals it may be more impactful to paint an exciting vision of the future rather than dwell on the problems of the past.

- *Be consistent in your judgements.* All managers and leaders face difficult disciplinary judgements in their careers; some will face many. When considering a disciplinary issue, think about at what stage of the transgression the individual was caught – after the fact or before it? Consider how Caruso's research might affect how you judge the severity of the misdemeanour.

- *Act now, ask questions later.* The more Machiavellian reader may consider this psychological insight an opportunity. If you face a potentially tricky issue, you might find that it is better to press ahead with a decision and consider the consequences later; your actions might be viewed more favourably with the benefit of hindsight.

What you might say about this

'Just because they were *planning* to call in sick falsely doesn't make it any worse than if they had already done so and I didn't know about it at the time.'

'Don't focus on the past. People are more excited by the future.'

'Just do it. We can always rationalise why afterwards.'

Where you can find out more

'When the future feels worse than the past: A temporal inconsistency in moral judgement', E. Caruso, *Journal of Experimental Psychology: General*, Vol. 139, No. 4, 2010.

IDEA #53
Want to win? Start by losing (a little)

Being informed that you are slightly behind a competitor can give the vital motivational spur needed to overcome them.

What you need to know

Losing during a competition is surely never a good thing. However, Jonah Berger of the Wharton School and Devin Pope of the Booth School of Business have turned this near truism on its head with a revelatory finding: under certain circumstances, individuals, groups and teams who are trailing opponents at a given point in a competition can actually receive a motivational boost from being behind, to the extent that they are more likely to win than if they had been ahead throughout. Analysing data from more than 18,000 professional National Basketball Association (NBA) games, they found that, at the half-time point, teams one point down were *more likely to win* than teams one point ahead. These findings were consistent – although less pronounced – with similar analyses they conducted for more than 45,000 collegiate basketball games and in laboratory studies where they found that participants in a repetitive keyboard-pressing game would increase their effort if told they were 'slightly behind' their competitors. In the keyboard-pressing studies, the authors were able to demonstrate that the positive motivational impact of being 'slightly behind' is more marked for individuals with higher self-efficacy (defined as the belief that one can achieve desired outputs) than those with low self-efficacy, although the positive impact was nonetheless apparent in both categories of participants.

Why it matters

Knowing how to motivate others is a vital trait in business. In seeking to explain human motivation through the prism of the latest advances in the biological and social sciences, two Harvard Business School professors – Paul Lawrence and Nitin Nohria – have suggested that humans possess four basic drives: acquiring objects and experiences; bonding with others in a mutually beneficial manner; learning about ourselves and the world we inhabit; and defending ourselves and ones dear to us. The last of these 'drives' chimes with the research of Berger and Pope, which shows that we seek to defend what is ours through competitive endeavour.

How this will change the way you work

- *Play mind games.* It may not be a tactic to use all the time, but sometimes, letting your team or star performer know they are 'a bit behind on the deadline' or 'so and so has been slightly outperforming you lately', might provide a brilliant motivational spur for them.

- *Keep things realistic.* It is crucial to remember that the motivational impact only occurs if the recipient of the intended spur genuinely is only slightly behind and thus can actually achieve their goal. If the suggested goal is unattainable this may in fact end up being demotivating and lead individuals to question their own ability if they fail to achieve the goal.

What you might say about this

'The other team's sales figures are better than ours, but there's still time to overtake them. We can do this!'

'You can turn this around. I believe in you.'

'We can't get complacent. I know our performance figures are healthy at the moment, but any slack and we'll get overtaken. The other departments will be trying twice as hard now.'

Where you can find out more

Paul Lawrence and Nitin Nohria, *Driven: How Human Nature Shapes Organizations*, Jossey-Bass, 2002.

'Can losing lead to winning?', Jonah Berger and Devin Pope, *Management Science*, Vol. 57, No. 5, 2011.

IDEA #54
Working on an acquisition? Seller, beware!

Too much trust during acquisitions can lead to sellers losing out.

What you need to know

It is a near gospel mantra that trust is the key to success in business. From making teams more harmonious to improving client–customer relationships, we are told by guru after guru that to get anywhere you need to be trusted. A number of studies have shown the impact that trust can have in business and, in particular, in smoothing over potentially fraught corporate buy-outs, but what happens if trust doesn't exist in a relationship? That's the question Melissa Graebner sought to answer when she analysed eight acquisitions where six publicly traded and two privately held companies of between 150 and 50,000 employees sought to purchase firms of between 20 and 335 workers. The average value of the deals was a hefty $175 million and all deals were full equity takeovers, although only half were successfully completed. Through more than 80 interviews with players in the transactions, Graebner uncovered the power of trust asymmetries in M&A transactions and how there is an imbalance in trust levels between buyers and sellers. In particular, Graebner's research showed how:

- buyers were less trusting than sellers; and
- buyers were more likely to deceive sellers than the reverse.

For example, buyers gave details of post-acquisition plans that stated there would be minimal lay-offs or workers would not have to relocate, only to completely renege on these assertions later. Sellers, by contrast, were far less likely to 'materially' deceive buyers – the worst they might do would be to engage in 'negotiation-related bluffing'; in others words, suggest that there were competing offers on the table for a company when there may not have been. On the whole, though, sellers were far more trusting of buyers – sometimes with significant negative consequences for the smaller party.

Why it matters

In an economic situation where mergers and acquisitions are becoming less common, takeovers are even more stressful for managers than ever before. Graebner's research suggests sellers are surprisingly trustworthy when it comes to being acquired – but wrongly so. Part of the explanation for their trusting nature is that sellers – by virtue of being comparatively small organisations – have fewer resources to spend on financial consultants or legal advice. But even when external counsel was brought in, it seems that sellers were nonetheless prone to turn a blind eye to caution and think the best of their prospective buyers. Buyers, on the other hand – perhaps more experienced in the M&A game and therefore battle-worn – had little problem justifying their deceptions. Graebner suggests that the buyers' fear of being deceived led them to justify their deceptive behaviour towards sellers.

How this will change the way you work

- The sad but simplest piece of advice here is simply to be less trusting. Sellers should always make sure that any post-integration promises a buyer makes should be contractually enforced – simply giving one's word is not good enough. Trust is a beautiful thing, but it can often be misplaced.

What you might say about this

'In my working relationship what trust asymmetries do I have?'

'We're being naïve and too trusting.'

'I need to see it in writing.'

Where you can find out more

'Caveat venditor: Trust asymmetries in acquisition of entrepreneurial firms', Melissa E. Graebner, *Academy of Management Journal*, Vol. 52, No. 3, 2009.

'Buyouts, information asymmetry and the family management dyad', C. Howorth, P. Westhead and M. Wright, *Journal of Business Venturing*, Vol. 19, No. 4, 2004.

David H. Maister, Robert Galford and Charles H. Green, *The Trusted Advisor*, Free Press, 2002.

IDEA #55
How social networks share knowledge

How knowledge-sharing in organisations is affected by social ties.

What you need to know

How close are you to your colleagues? Relationships between individuals in social networks have often been characterised as being either 'strong social ties' or 'weak social ties'. In 1973 the sociologist Mark Granovetter argued that the strength or weakness of a tie is a determined by 'a combination of the amount of time [spent in interaction], the emotional intensity, the intimacy, and the reciprocal services which characterise the tie [between individuals]'.

Prior to Granovetter's work, scholars believed that strong ties would be invariably beneficial to organisations and lead to improvements in morale, inter-group coordination, innovation and knowledge-sharing. Granovetter demonstrated that while strong ties may encourage individuals to share knowledge and information with those they hold ties with, this was to the detriment of those outside the strong social ties; they are often ignored and information not shared with them.

Why it matters

More recently, Morten Hansen – in a highly cited article for *Administrative Science Quarterly* – analysed the relationship between social network ties, knowledge-sharing and product development in a large electronics company. Hansen built on Granovetter's work, but added a subtle nuance to his conclusion: the positive or negative impact of social network tie strength is dependent on the complexity of knowledge being transferred. Consequently, where the knowledge being transferred was reasonably simple (e.g., 'how do I record my expenses?'), in Hansen's analysis weak ties were most effective. This was because with weak ties, usually the acquirer of the information was being told something new and, thus, knowledge transferred across team was 'non-redundant' (i.e., useful). Strong ties, by contrast could lead to teams asking those they already knew well for information they already knew about! However, where the knowledge sought was complex to transfer (e.g., 'how do I record a macro to join a dozen spreadsheet models together?'), a problem arose because organisations with weak social ties are often poor at codifying knowledge and, in turn, this makes it harder to share. Strong ties, on the other hand, often lead to good codification of knowledge and this makes sharing knowledge easier.

How this will change the way you work

- Internal Wiki or stick to email? Heavy-handed document and version control or keep stuff stored in your inbox? Weekly team meetings in person or quarterly written updates? How you choose to try and mould social network ties in your organisation or team should – in part – take into consideration what type of activities you undertake.

- If innovation and creativity is what you specialise in, weak social ties – in other words, discouraging the formation of small and introverted teams – might be a good strategy.

- If transferring complex knowledge across your organisation is key, then strong social ties – perhaps formed through centralised knowledge management databases and frequent team-building events – could help.

What you might say about this

'A small group of employees who seem to be best friends and go out together frequently may paint a disproportionate picture of how sociable our company actually is – what about all our other staff?'

'How we facilitate our employees engaging with each other will have an impact on how successfully we transfer knowledge and best practice across the company.'

'I've noticed some cliques forming in the office – small close networks might be positive if we're trying to share complex information but in terms of creating a universal shared working style these cliques could hold us back.'

Where you can find out more

'The strength of weak ties', Mark S. Granovetter, *American Journal of Sociology*, Vol. 78, No. 6, 1973.

'The search–transfer problem: The role of weak ties in sharing knowledge across organization subunits', Morten T. Hansen, *Administrative Science Quarterly*, Vol. 44, No. 1, 1999.

IDEA #56
I'm in charge – check my paycheque

When pay disparity can improve team outcomes.

What you need to know

Led by Nir Halevy, assistant professor of organisational behaviour at Stanford Graduate School of Business, a team of researchers investigated the impact of pay dispersion (i.e., pay disparities within teams) on the performance of American National Basketball Association (NBA) teams between 1997 and 2007. Previous research on dispersion has suggested that wide financial disparities (or operational disparities – e.g., some team members have more playing time than others) create a sense of hierarchy that hurts commitment, cooperation and performance in teams. However, Halevy *et al.*'s research found that, in basketball, 'pay dispersion and starting line-up dispersion were significant predictors of increased intragroup co-ordination and co-operation, and enhanced the performance of professional basketball teams'. Given that considerable research has successfully shown the opposite effect of pay dispersion in baseball, this led the researchers to an interesting conclusion. They suggest that, in instances where teams require strong 'procedural interdependence' (i.e., working together closely – such as in basketball) to succeed, pay dispersion can have a positive impact on team performance. However, in team circumstances where 'procedural independence' (i.e., individual performance matters the most – such as baseball) is key, pay disparity has a negative impact.

Why it matters

How does your organisation deal with sharing salary levels? Whether you try and keep it a secret or not, it is an inevitability of team-working that members will find out who earns most and who earns least. The impact of this is that – consciously or not – organisational hierarchies are formed based on financial disparities. Depending on what your organisation does, hierarchies may help or hinder performance.

How this will change the way you work

- What type of teams do you work in? In order to ascertain whether hierarchies are having a positive or negative effect on performance, first consider whether your tasks are governed by 'procedural interdependence' or 'procedural independence'. In the case of the former, make sure everyone knows what their roles and responsibilities are – who reports to who and how the team is meant to work together. In team sports such as football, which are highly procedurally interdependent, the manager or coach is in charge with the captain as their spokesperson on the field – clear responsibilities and hierarchies help to ensure smooth performance.

- In procedurally independent sports such as golf, the hierarchical lines are much less clear. Any attempt to impose organisational hierarchies is likely to result in deterioration in team performance.

- Similarly, if you run a team of highly autonomous fund managers, widely published pay disparities will probably cause a severe disruption to team harmony, as previously independent individuals may feel constrained by the hierarchies caused by the pay disparity.

What you might say about this

'The team is what matters, not the individuals.'

'It's not wise for us to have large pay disparities – it will hurt team harmony.'

'To function well we need to have a clear understanding of who's in charge and who does what. This isn't a case of massaging egos, it's a case of working in the most effective manner possible.'

Where you can find out more

'When hierarchy wins: Evidence from the National Basketball Association', N. Halevy, E. Chou, A. Galinsky and J.K. Murnighan, *Social Psychological and Personality Science*, Vol. 3, No. 4, 2012.

IDEA #57
Great performance, but I regress

Extreme performance is rarely permanent.

What you need to know

Why do some football players have one tremendous season only to follow it with a mediocre one? By the same token, why is it that one fund manager can average exceptional returns one year, only to have a disastrous one the next? The answer – a lot of the time at least – can be found in a statistical quirk known as 'regression to the mean' (RTTM).

Why it matters

Sir Francis Galton popularised the term in the 1880s through a paper on the subject (incidentally, the paper incorrectly theorised why

RTTM occurs, but his observations were still valid). Galton wondered why an extreme physical characteristic – such as being very tall – is not always passed down from a parent to child. The answer lies in the fact that if you take an extreme observation (such as: a very tall parent; a season where a football striker scored an unusually high number of goals; an exceptionally poor test score) and then measure the same observation again, you will almost always find the extreme observation has disappeared. This is because the first extreme observation was very rare (and hence unlikely) so the likelihood of it happening again is very low. In crude terms, lightning rarely strikes twice.

How this will change the way you work

- Understand the limitations of 'average performance'. Recognising the potential pitfalls of RTTM can have profound implications for how we work. To take an obvious example, any good project manager knows that to make an improvement happen, first you need to measure baseline performance and then set targets to better this. What if your baseline doesn't take account of RTTM? For example, you often hear 'success stories' that go something like, 'at our worst, we were operating at a utilisation rate of 24 per cent, but since our project started we've got utilisation up to a high of 87 per cent.' Because this story refers to two extremes, it's hard to tell what the real improvement was. It's likely that 24 per cent was a period of extremely low performance – and RTTM tells us that it is likely to have risen without any action the next time utilisation was measured. Similarly, 87 per cent may be an extremely high data point and, if measured again, we might expect a lower figure.

- Remember the real performance improvement is still possible. It's important to note that RTTM doesn't mean improvements in performance don't happen, only, if you take an unusually low or high measurement of something, because it's hard to measure things precisely and exclude things such as luck or fortune, this figure will be unrepresentative of 'true performance'. A better alternative is to take the longer-term view of things and use rolling averages.

What you might say about this

'He had a terrible project. We had words and his next project was great. Did I improve things or was that just regression to the mean?'

'This hedge fund has had one exceptional year of returns. Is it skill or luck?'

'We need to be careful of factoring in regression to the mean when monitoring progress against targets, but that doesn't mean we should underplay any improvements in performance – RTTM is an observation about data, not a causal factor in performance.'

Where you can find out more

'Regression towards the mean and the study of change', John R. Nesselroade, Stephen M. Stigler and Paul B. Baltes, *Psychological Bulletin*, Vol. 88, No. 3, 1980.

'Regression towards mediocrity in hereditary stature', Francis Galton, *The Journal of the Anthropological Institute of Great Britain and Ireland*, Vol. 15, 1886.

IDEA #58
A bird in the hand is worth two in the bush

How we evaluate decisions varies according to timescales.

What you need to know

Consider the following: would you rather receive £10 now or £12 in a year's time? Now consider this issue: you have a big work presentation tomorrow that you're nervous about and would happily delay, but when asked if you'd like to delay it a month ago, you said no. Both these scenarios are common examples of quirks in how we make decisions. The first example elucidates the issue of 'intertemporal choice' – how we value something at different points in time. The second example covers 'time inconsistency' – how our preferences for a particular decision change over time. Both have important implications for how we work and live.

Why it matters

Making decisions about the future is something we have to do all the time yet we are consistently bad at it. How often have you chosen a burger over a salad or stayed in and watched TV as opposed to going for a run in the cold? In short, we are biased to favouring short-term rewards over long-term gains. In one startling survey of 400 CFOs, four-fifths of respondents stated they would reduce current marketing and product development expenditure even if it compromised long-term performance. From magnetic resonance imaging, we know that different parts of our brains deal with time-based decisions differently and more often than not it is the part of the brain that errs towards short-term decisions (the limbic system) that wins. As a result, we are prone to making poor decisions that value the immediate over the long-term.

How this will change the way you work

- Economists have traditionally accounted for the difficulty in balancing the short-term with the long-term through discounted utility models. In finance, for example, many investment decisions are based on net present value calculations, which seek to determine the financial value of an option over a long period of time. In practice, this is often too complex a method to use on a day-to-day basis and many decisions we have to make (e.g., 'Should I buy a new television now or wait a year till this model is cheaper?') are still not easily solved through this means (for example, how do you calculate the internal rate of return for spending money on buying a new television?) The best we can hope to do to overcome our bias is simply to be aware of it.

- The next time you are confronted with a decision involving a short-term and long-term trade-off, remember you'll be predisposed to favouring the short-term one. Question why and make sure your logic stands up in your reasoning. If it doesn't, you might want to change your mind.

What you might say about this

'Any offer we make to customers should focus on providing them with short-term rewards; they'll value them more highly than long-term ones.'

'That might be the right answer now, but we should think about whether it will still be so in a year's time.'

'Short-term pain for long-term gain.'

Where you can find out more

'Separate neural systems value immediate and delayed monetary rewards', Samuel M. McClure, David I. Laibson, George Loewenstein and Jonathan D. Cohen, *Science*, Vol. 306, 2004.

'Value destruction and financial reporting decisions', John Graham, Campbell Harvey and Shiva Rajgopal, *Financial Analysts Journal*, Vol. 62, No. 6, 2006.

Finn E. Kydland and Edward C. Prescott, 'Rules rather than discretion: The inconsistency of optimal plans', *Journal of Political Economy*, Vol. 85, No. 3, 1977.

IDEA #59
The hidden evil of stereotype threats

Negative stereotypes can severely hamper the performance and prospects of minority groups.

What you need to know

Asians are good at maths. Women can't drive. Old people have bad memories. Stereotypes – in the workplace and outside it – abound. Yet, beyond the realm of risqué jokes or flippant comments, negative stereotypes can have a very real, and very detrimental, impact on those on the receiving end. Spearheaded by the Stanford-based social psychologist, Claude Steele, a huge body of research has built up over the past 20 years demonstrating the impact of negative stereotypes in a variety of academic and non-academic settings.

An example of a stereotype threat is where an individual – usually, although not exclusively, from a minority group – is made conscious of a negative, commonly held, stereotype perception of that group. For instance, in one experiment, women performed significantly worse in a mathematics test when they took the test alongside men than when they took it only alongside other women. Here, the negative stereotype was that 'women are bad at maths' and it was hypothesised that the participants were made aware of the stereotype (consciously or subconsciously) by the presence of men taking the test.

Why it matters

Studies have shown that stereotype threats can have a negative impact in a range of settings, including: the superiority of men over women at negotiating; or that Caucasian men are worse at maths than Asian men. In each instance, participants from the stereotyped group performed worse at the task under evaluation when they were made aware of the stereotype than when the issue of the stereotype was not raised.

How this will change the way you work

- Think big, act small. Happily, research has demonstrated that small interventions can have a large impact on reducing the negative effects of stereotype threat. Perhaps the most unexpected successful intervention is to encourage self-affirmation. An example of this is to ask individuals to spend some time thinking and writing about a value that matters to them prior to undertaking a specific task. In a 2006 experiment to this end, the grades of African-American students were significantly improved and the achievement gap between them and non-African-American students was bridged by 40 per cent through this simple action. By helping individuals realise their own values and self-worth, it is possible to overcome their internal fears regarding stereotypes that may be held about them.

What you might say about this

'I know about the existence of stereotype threat so I'm not going to let it affect me.'

'What positive stereotypes can we help reinforce?'

'Before you take this assessment, I'd like you to spend some time thinking about the personal value you most cherish.'

Where you can find out more

Claude Steele, *Whistling Vivaldi: and Other Clues to How Stereotypes Affect Us*, W.W. Norton & Company, 2010.

'Reducing stereotype threat in order to facilitate learning', Kathryn L. Boucher, Robert Rydell, Katie Van Loo and Michael Rydell, *European Journal of Social Psychology*, Vol. 42, No. 2, 2012.

'Reducing the racial achievement gap: A social-psychological intervention', G.L. Cohen, J. Garcia, N. Apfel and A. Master, *Science*, Vol. 313, No. 5791, 2006.

IDEA #60
How to turn that black swan white

Highly improbable events can have the biggest impact on the world.

What you need to know

Nassim Nicholas Taleb, a former hedge fund manager and Wall Street trader who has turned his hand to academia, decries mankind's seemingly insatiable – but ultimately flawed – appetite for trying to predict the future. Criticising a gamut of high-profile individuals, from risk managers to politicians to Nobel laureates, Taleb has suggested that modern attitudes towards risk, uncertainty and predicting the future are worthless because they hero-worship the Gaussian normal distribution 'bell curve' view of the world where the 'average' rules. Instead, Taleb encourages a more 'fat-tailed' (see Idea #63) conception of risk; where the outliers and unexpected events still matter.

Taleb's critical theory is that unexpected and unpredictable events have the biggest impact on mankind, yet precisely because they are unexpected and unpredictable, little attention is paid to mitigate their risks. These events, such as 9/11 or the 2008 global financial crash, are Taleb's 'black swans' – a term borrowed from a popular London phrase of the early modern period that 'all swans must be white', since at the time there was no evidence to the contrary. Black swan events have three main characteristics: they are almost entirely unexpected; they have a huge (positive or negative) impact; and, hubristically, society seeks to make them appear predictable *post facto*, even though nobody foresaw their coming.

Why it matters

A prime example of a black swan event is the collapse of the Long-Term Capital Management hedge fund in 1998. The managers of the fund were utterly convinced by the precision and accuracy of their elaborate models, to the extent that their reliance on them meant when real-world events occurred which the models did not take account of (the models were focused on events occurring within a limited range of likelihood), they were unable to effectively deal with the fall out, such as with the 1997 Asian financial crisis.

Similarly, many hospitals operate patient discharge plans on the premise that the 'average' patient stays, say, three days in hospital. This plan might enable patients to flow in and out of hospital without blocking up expensive and highly prized beds, yet, if a large, unexpected number of patients end up requiring 30-day stays, the patient flow plan is utterly disrupted and the hospital is them under severe pressure to operate safely. An over-reliance on predictive models and an acute focus on the mean type of activity (or deviations within this) can lead to disaster.

How this will change the way you work

- *Recognise the drawbacks.* In the first instance, an appreciation of the limitations of predictive modelling is sensible. Many companies will have five-year financial projections, often to ludicrously precise decimal places. Rather than believe blindly in these plans, it is more sensible to give a range of potential scenarios, then humbly and realistically acknowledge the many 'unknown unknowns'.

- *Keep it simple.* There is a need to simplify and compartmentalise most processes and products. The more complex a product (financial derivatives such as collateralised debt obligations (CDOs) being a case in point), the more likely it is to have unknown associated risks that are hard to mitigate. The more interlinked processes are (with financial markets being a prime case in point) the easier it is for black swan events to multiply their effect in magnitude and gravity.

- *Watch out for the lucky swan.* On a more positive note, appreciate the fact that some black swans can have a positive effect – the internet, for example. You should seek to make yourself available to be the lucky recipient of these, by ensuring you expose yourself to a healthy amount of positive uncertainty. Surround yourself with varied and innovative potential commercial partners – you never know what opportunities may arise from this.

What you might say about this

'Events always seem more obvious in hindsight – we really didn't see it coming.'

'Everything we do assumes the world has a neat, normal distribution. What if it doesn't?'

'I'd love to say otherwise, but I genuinely just don't know.'

Where you can find out more

Nassim Nicholas Taleb, *The Black Swan: The Impact of the Highly Improbable*, Penguin: Allen Lane, 2007.

IDEA #61
Kick the habit

How individuals and organisations can break out of their bad habits.

What you need to know

Over the past ten years, an increasingly sophisticated body of research has built up around habits. According to studies led by Wendy Wood of the University of Southern California 'approximately 45 per cent of everyday behaviours tend to be repeated in the same location every day'. These behaviours are, in other words, habits – undertaken largely unthinkingly by us, but they take up a tremendous amount of our lives. Charles DuHigg, a *New York Times* reporter has investigated the scientific research behind habits in considerable detail and his book, *The Power of Habit*, has explained what it is that causes habits (both good and bad) in individuals and organisations and how we can change them.

Why it matters

From dangerous personal problems such as alcohol addiction to trivial organisational ones such as copying everyone in on office emails, repeated behaviours are formed by the three-stage 'habit loop':

- *the cue* – the trigger for the behaviour;
- *the routine* – the behavioural actions; and
- *the reward* – a usually positive recognition of the behaviour, which helps your brain embed the habit to make it even easier to repeat in future.

DuHigg uses his (former) proclivity for biscuits to show how this works in practice. Around mid-afternoon at work he would feel an urge for a biscuit (the cue – cues are usually governed by a certain time, place, action, person or frame of mind); he would walk to the cafeteria to buy a biscuit (the routine); then eat the biscuit (the reward).

Thankfully – as several studies have demonstrated – it is possible to break out of habits, although it's much harder to remove them completely. For example, as DuHigg sought to break out of his biscuit habit, he analysed his 'habit loop' and realised that the *real* reward he prized from his habit was socialising with his colleagues as he got up to purchase his biscuit from the cafeteria. He could achieve this reward through other means, by changing his routine to buying an apple from the cafeteria, for instance. Alcoholics Anonymous (AA) works using a similar method – alcoholism is usually driven by stress (cue), leading to drinking (routine), leading to a reduction in or forgetting of one's anxieties through the effects of alcohol (reward). The AA helps individuals keep the cue and reward, but changes the routine to socialising with other individuals to help them contextualise and share their anxieties instead of drinking.

DuHigg caused a stir with a *New York Times* article that demonstrated how major companies track our habits. His research suggested that the US retailer Target uses transaction data from customers to pinpoint when young women are pregnant – often before they have even told any family or friends – and then uses this information to offer them special promotions of pregnancy products. Research has shown that major life changes (such as pregnancies or divorces) cause habits to become 'flexible' – in other words, individuals are more prone to changing or breaking their well-worn habits. This moment in time is a prime opportunity to incentivise them to get into new habits – such as buying Target products.

How this will change the way you work

- *Small change, big impact.* DuHigg also suggests that managers and leaders can go a long way to changing company cultures through inducing small habit changes in employees that in turn lead to large-scale cultural change. DuHigg cites examples such as Paul O'Neill at the aluminium manufacturer Alcoa, who transformed the company's safety record by making employees prioritise safety in everything they did, or Howard Schultz at Starbucks, who made excellent customer service in frontline staff his priority. The concluding message is clear: small habit change can have a big impact. Using the cue–routine–reward 'habit loop', think about what habits you either want to break or make in your life.

What you might say about this

'Lao Tzu was right: "Watch your habits; they become your character. Watch your character, it becomes your destiny."'

'What matters first and foremost is what we do now, because that will determine where we go in the future. I want us to work out our company habits and see which we need to change.'

'I want to go to the gym more. I need to work out the "habit loop" I need to create to make this happen.'

Where you can find out more

'Habits – a repeat performance', David T. Neal, Wendy Wood and Jeffrey M. Quinn, *Current Directions in Psychological Science*, Vol. 15, No. 4, 2006.

Charles DuHigg, *The Power of Habit: Why We Do What We Do in Life and Business*, Random House, 2012.

IDEA #62
The biology of risk-taking

Two hormones – testosterone and cortisol – have a huge effect on how we work.

What you need to know

John Coates, a derivatives trader turned Cambridge University neuroscientist, was fascinated by the biological processes at work on his old hunting ground of the trading floor. He has identified two key hormones that have a huge impact on how we work: testosterone, which feeds our appetite for risk; and cortisol, which inhibits our appetite for risk.

In a 2005 study, Coates took saliva samples from 250 traders (all but three of whom were male) over a two-week period and tracked the outcomes of their trades. Incredibly, Coates found a strong correlation: when testosterone levels were particularly high in the morning, traders made more money later that day than if testosterone levels were low. On an annualised basis, Coates calculated the difference between a high-testosterone and low-testosterone day to be worth up to $1m. Fluctuations in testosterone levels (which are much more relevant to men and, specifically, young men – the prevalent demographic in most trading firms) can consequently have a huge impact on attitudes to risk. A spiralling cycle of testosterone can occur – known as the 'winner effect' – whereby high levels of testosterone encourage risk-tasking; if the risks are rewarded, this generates yet more testosterone and, subsequently, greater risk-taking.

The flip-side of this is when a large, unexpected loss is experienced. In this instance, another hormone – cortisol – kicks in. Cortisol is a hormone that helps the body deal with threats; it leads to a shutting down of the digestive system and the breakdown of glucose previously stored by the body. Essentially, the body tries to protect itself by shutting down. One of the by-products of this is that the appetite for risk collapses. As abnormal levels of hormones affect the body and the parts of our brains that govern rationality, we become more susceptible to emotional, and potentially irrational, decision-making.

Why it matters

It is not hard to see the potential implications of testosterone and cortisol levels in financial markets and economic cycles. When male traders are reaping financial rewards, they are generating increasing levels of testosterone in the process – a bull market is underway. By contrast, when trading is generating losses, cortisol abounds. Physiologically, traders' bodies become swamped with cortisol, increasing their desire to protect what they have and reducing their appetite for taking risks. A bear market, in other words. The conventional, rational economic assumptions that govern the functioning of financial markets gloss over the potential impact of physiological changes in the marketplace. Coates' research and the developing field of neuroeconomics can help add a much richer understanding of what really happens on the trading floor.

How this will change the way you work

- *Change the hormonal make-up of the workplace.* One of Coates' suggestions to combat the effects of hormones on the trading floor is simple: hire fewer young men and more women and older men, both of whom are less susceptible to volatile fluctuations in testosterone levels. A paper from 2001 suggests there may be other benefits to hiring more women. This demonstrated that females at a large discount brokerage had significantly better returns on common stock investments than their male counterparts.

- *Reward the long-term.* Much of the effects of testosterone and cortisol are exacerbated by the short-term nature of trading; annual profits are prized more greatly than returns over a, say, five-year period. Change reward mechanisms to encourage a longer-term perspective and thereby reduce the pressure to take high, short-term risks.

- *Delay your response.* Any significant financial loss or gain is likely to stimulate an impact on the body, the impact of which we are still working out. Given the evidence that hormonal fluctuations can encourage us to think and act irrationally, it may make sense to put a time delay on any actions taken after an unexpected event. This applies outside of the financial world too. If, for example, you receive an unpleasant email from a colleague, stop yourself from responding straight away. Once the initial emotional impact has abated, you might feel differently about how you'd like to respond. Putting a timer delay on sending your emails can help in this respect too.

What you might say about this

'I'm being emotional about this. I need to calm down.'

'What do we think is the behavioural impact of our company's demographic profile?'

'You need to take a break.'

Where you can find out more

John Coates, *The Hour Between Dog and Wolf: Risk Taking, Gut Feelings and the Biology of Boom and Bust*, Fourth Estate, 2012.

'Boys will be boys: Gender, overconfidence, and common stock investment', Brad M. Barber and Terrance Odean, *The Quarterly Journal of Economics*, February 2001.

IDEA #63
Do you have a Pareto or a long tail?

The Internet has changed the supply and demand of products in fundamental ways.

What you need to know

The Pareto distribution – commonly known as the '80/20 principle' – is surely one of the most popularly repeated 'rules' in business. The term, named after the Italian economist who first observed it, refers to the frequent observation that 20 per cent of one thing is usually responsible for 80 per cent of another. For instance, Vilfredo Pareto observed that, at the start of the twentieth century in his native Italy, 20 per cent of individuals owned 80 per cent of the country's wealth. Managers across the world have adopted this theory to claim that '20 per cent of the work leads to 80 per cent of the impact' or '20 per cent of products are responsible for 80 per cent of revenue'.

Until the advent of the Internet, most retailers' income streams conformed to a Pareto distribution. However, as Chris Anderson – editor-in-chief of *Wired* magazine – has argued, this is no longer the case. Major retailers' revenues – such as Amazon's – conform to a 'long-tail' distribution. Plotted as a graph, many values would stretch far away to the right of the mean. In other words, Amazon makes more of its revenue from selling lots of low-volume items, than they do from a small number of high-volume sale products.

Why it matters

Traditionally, businesses have sought to make economies by making or selling a small number of highly desirable products or services to a large number of customers. This is frequently seen in a variety of environments. Investment funds try to minimise their investor numbers to focus effort on 'high-value' customers; carmakers focus on producing a small number of highly popular models of automobile; and governments raise the majority of tax receipts from the wealthiest citizens.

The main reason for this is simple economics: there are economies of scale to be found in concentrating efforts on a small number of areas. Storing products that few people buy or creating cars that nobody wants is expensive and wasteful. However the Internet is changing this. Demand for hard-to-find items has risen as it is easier to search for rare products than ever before, and the supply of these products has increased thanks to the advent of providers such as Amazon whose business model relies on cheap centralised warehousing and distribution supply chains. The age of the 'long tail' may be upon us.

How this will change the way you work

- *Embrace the long tail:* Few industries are likely to escape the impact of the move towards long-tail distributions. As a consequence, you should either embrace the long tail or prepare to defend yourself from it.

- *Embrace the future.* If your customers are likely to want increasingly uncommon and specialised products, make it cheaper and easier for your organisation to provide them. Lower your costs of inventory and storage of goods through centralised warehousing or sharing storage space with other retailers. Reach out to new customer groups at the tail of the distribution by using cheaper marketing methods through social networks or viral marketing campaigns.

- *Protect your turf.* Alternatively, if branching out into markets further down the tail is neither economically viable nor strategically desirable, make sure that your offering is so good all the choice in the world of competitor products does not compare with your proposition. Think about what makes your product or service uniquely different and how can you protect this from increased competition.

What you might say about this

'What about the 80 per cent of the market we haven't traditionally focused on? How can we make it financially sensible to target them?'

'The Internet is increasing competition for us – how can we protect ourselves from this?'

'Do we want to be a niche provider or a mass market provider? We can't just lie somewhere in the middle and hope for the best.'

Where you can find out more

'Goodbye Pareto principle, hello long tail: The effect of search costs on the concentration of product sales', Erik Brynjolfsson, Yu Jeffrey Hu and Duncan Simester, *Management Science*, Vol. 57, No. 8, 2011.

Chris Anderson, *The Long Tail: Why the Future of Business is Selling Less of More*, Hyperion, 2006.

IDEA #64
Six seconds to land your dream job

Make your CV as decluttered as possible because nobody will read it for very long.

What you need to know

In 1962 the Russian psychologist and expert in the study of eye tracking, Alfred Yarbus, wrote that where we gaze during a task is 'dependent not only on what is shown on the [thing facing us], but also on the problem facing the observer and the information that he hopes to gain [from that which he is observing]'. In other words, where we look is determined by where we expect to find things. So far, so obvious, but we rarely think through the practical implications of this.

Why it matters

Take an industry where 'observers' are time-poor and there is no shortage of willing individuals who wish to be 'observed': recruitment. Recruiters often have a stream of CVs to screen for potential candidates and little time to do this effectively. So how do they prioritise their time and what do they look for in CVs? Using eye-tracking technology, the New York-based recruitment company The Ladders ran an experiment tracking how 30 recruiters evaluated CVs over a ten-week period. Somewhat worryingly, the study found that recruiters spend on average *six seconds* (6.25 seconds mean; 5.3 seconds median) looking at an individual CV – either paper copies or on online platforms such as LinkedIn. During these few seconds, recruiters spent 80 per cent of their time looking at:

- Candidate's name
- Current company – role title
- Previous company – role title
- Current position start and end dates
- Previous position start and end dates
- Education.

How this will change the way you work

- If you're looking for a job, it's vital that your CV is simple and clear. Make sure the key things recruiters are looking for stand out. Given the tiny amount of time that is devoted to CVs, most of your great achievements won't actually be read – most recruiters will go straight to the six points listed above and form their judgements on you through these.

- If you do have a particularly unusual and noteworthy past that doesn't easily fit into these six areas – you're an Olympic gold medallist or sold your first start-up as a teenager for several million quid – make sure this is particularly visible on the CV; either at the top of the CV or embedded into one of the six key areas. Otherwise it risks being ignored in the rush of evaluation.

What you might say about this

'I need to make my CV as easy as possible for a recruiter to read.'

'I should make my CV smart, clean and clear – extraneous information will just waste the precious little time a recruiter will spend evaluating it.'

'You shouldn't risk a funky new design format. A recruiter is used to looking in standard places for information – if you change this around, they won't know where to look for your key information.'

Where you can find out more

Alfred L. Yarbus, *Eye Movements and Vision*, Plenum Press, 1967.

'Eye-tracking online metacognition: Cognitive complexity and recruiter decision-making', Will Evans, *The Ladders*, 2012.

IDEA #65
Tell stories, not facts

Stories and narratives have far more impact than numbers.

What you need to know

What's the best way to make a lasting impact with your message? Charities seeking donations are continuously striving to encourage individuals to part with their cash to do good for others. An experiment conducted at the Wharton School highlighted how facts and data have less of an impact on potential donors than raw human stories.

Students were given $5 to complete a short survey, and then shown a flyer requesting a donation to a major global children's charity. There were two different groups of students, each shown a different flyer.

The first group's flyer noted that, 'food shortages in Malawi are affecting more than three million children. In Zambia, severe rainfall deficits have resulted in a 42 per cent drop in maize production from 2000. As a result, an estimated three million Zambians face hunger.

Four million Angolans … have been forced to flee their homes. More than 11 million people in Ethiopia need immediate food assistance.'

The second group's flyer contained a picture of a young girl and stated, 'any money that you donate will go to Rokia, a seven-year-old girl from Mali, Africa. Rokia is desperately poor and faces a threat of severe hunger or even starvation. Her life will be changed for the better as a result of your financial gift. With your support, and the support of other caring sponsors, Save the Children will work with Rokia's family and other members of the community to help feed her, provide her with education, as well as basic medical care and hygiene education.'

Revealingly, when asked for donations following reading the flyers, the first group donated an average of $1.16 per student and the second group donated an average of $2.83 per student.

Why it matters

While the first flyer contained clear, quantifiable and apparently compelling empirical evidence of the nature and scale of the problems the charity is trying to tackle, it elicited less than half the donations of the second flyer. The second flyer, by contrast, contained no numerical information (bar the age of Rokia), nor gave any indication of the size or scale of the problem. Through the prism of one young girl's plight – told both verbally and pictorially – the impact was more than twice as great as the text-heavy flyer. A simple, intelligible story was more powerful than a logical, empirical statement.

How this will change the way you work

- *Tell a story.* Leaders constantly have to describe what the future might look like: boards need to sign-off on strategy plans; investors and shareholders need to be confident of projected financial positions; teams and individuals need to know where their company is going. The most common medium used to communicate this is the analytical model, probably told through some PowerPoint slides, sometimes summarised in a dry press release. This is usually as inspiring and exciting as it sounds. The Wharton School's research suggests that, when communicating, you should aim to paint a story – maybe centred on a customer or an employee or investor – that resonates with the audience. This need not be at the expense of the detailed modelling and analysis. Rather, the story should be a compelling synthesis of what your empirically formed projections are suggesting.

What you might say about this

'In our hospital of the future, Mr Smith won't have to travel back and forth for repeated tests – he'll receive the best-quality treatment quickly and safely in one visit to us.'

'Let's do some future planning: I want you to write a paragraph from the perspective of your future self in ten years' time, looking back on all the great things you've achieved. What does she say?'

'Ladies and gentlemen, you can read all the details of our business plan and projections later. Today, I just want to tell you about the vision of our company, as told from the viewpoint of one of our customers.'

Where you can find out more

'Sympathy and callousness: The impact of deliberative thought on donations to identifiable and statistical victims', Deborah A. Small, George Loewenstein and Paul Slovic, *Organizational Behavior and Human Decision Processes*, Vol. 102, No. 2, 2007.

IDEA #66
How to avoid buying a lemon

Information asymmetry leads to inefficient and ineffective markets.

What you need to know

Consider the used car market, where ownership of vehicles is transferred from a seller to a buyer. In American slang, a 'cherry' is a good car (well-maintained) and a 'lemon' is a bad one (liable to break down soon after purchase). Because of the nature of the market, it is hard for buyers to ascertain whether a prospective purchase is a 'cherry' or a 'lemon'; variables such as the previous owner's driving style, accident history, maintenance checks and so on – which all contribute to the quality of the car – are difficult for the prospective buyer to gauge. The seller, however, knows all or most of this information. As a result there is an 'information asymmetry' in this market – one party in a transaction knows more relevant information than the other.

The effect of this in a used car market is stark. Initially, because it is difficult for buyers to assess a car's quality, some sellers will take advantage of this and put low-quality cars on the market at above-value prices. Over time, buyers will come to realise the risks of this and in turn this will drive down average prices in the market as buyers are unwilling to pay high amounts at the risk of purchasing a poor-quality car. Consequently, with average market prices depressed, sellers will be unwilling to sell high-quality cars because of the lower fees the market dictates for them. The bad effectively drives out the good.

Why it matters

The Nobel Prize-winning economist George Akerlof popularised the concept of the 'market for lemons' in his eponymous 1970 paper in the *Quarterly Journal of Economics*. Since then, the field of economics has been hugely influenced by his theory. Information asymmetry can be found virtually everywhere. For example, in health insurance, vendors know less about the current health of those being insured than the individuals purchasing the insurance; in house-selling, estate agents usually possess more knowledge about their prospective sales than home-seekers; in financial markets, some investors may possess greater knowledge than others.

As a side point about perseverance, Akerlof's game-changing paper was rejected by three prestigious journals on the grounds of being either incorrect or trivial before finding a home in the *Quarterly Journal of Economics*. It is now one of the most-cited economics papers of all time.

How this will change the way you work

- *Grant equal access.* The only way to truly break down information asymmetry is to ensure that all parties involved have equal access to the relevant knowledge and information. In practice, this is a solution policy-makers have grappled with to varying (but largely low) degrees of success for decades. In the US, the Magnuson–Moss Warranty Act (dubbed the 'lemon law' after Akerlof's allegorical paper) seeks to protect buyers in the used car market.

- *Make your differences transparent.* There is something beyond waiting for market regulations that individual companies can do to try and overcome information asymmetry: where companies hold more power than consumers, level the playing field. Increasingly supermarkets advertise 'price comparisons' with their rivals. If you offer better rates or a more compelling package than your competitors this may be a sensible option. If you don't offer a better alternative to your competitors, then perhaps you should!

What you might say about this

'What information asymmetries exist in our industry?'

'In the past we've made money out of the fact our customers are at the mercy of information asymmetry; with increasing market transparency, can we always rely on information asymmetry to give us an advantage over our competitors? Is it even ethical to do so?'

'I've just found out how much money they make from their customers. I'm never using them again.'

Where you can find out more

'The market for "lemons": Quality uncertainty and the market mechanism', George A. Akerlof, *Quarterly Journal of Economics*, Vol. 84, No. 3, 1970.

IDEA #67
Flawed headhunting

Stars in one organisation quickly fade out in another.

What you need to know

Boris Groysberg of Harvard Business School wanted to know the answer to the question 'can high-performing individuals successfully transfer their performance from one organisation to another?' Focusing on the performance of more than 20,000 Wall Street equity analysts – who are annually ranked by the trade journal *Institutional Investor* – from 1988 through to 1996, Groysberg's research teased out some fascinating insights. First, 'star analysts who switched employers paid a high price (in performance, not compensation) for jumping ship relative to comparable stars who stayed put'. Second, women were much less prone to deterioration in performance following a change in employment than men. Groysberg concluded that the more interesting question is thus, 'which stars are portable under which circumstances – and why?'

Why it matters

Building on a paper Groysberg published in the *Harvard Business Review* in 2006, he suggests that firms need to be a lot more strategic in their recruitment plans. It is too easy to be seduced by the 'winner's curse' – assuming that high performers in one organisation must translate into high performers in another. In reality, the data suggest that this is rarely the case. If you are looking to poach or entice stars, it would be wise to hire from firms that are similar in orientation to your own – and are of 'lesser or equivalent quality'.

How this will change the way you work

- From bringing in a new CEO, to building a new team, recruitment is an expensive and tricky business. Groysberg's theory of portability suggests there are certain skillsets that are easier to transfer than others. For example, skills that are focused on a specific company or a particular industry will only be useful if the individual in question is likely to move to a similar corporate culture or work within the same industry as before. Strategic skills such as cost-cutting or driving growth are more generic across firms, but will only be useful if the new working environment requires these talents to be tested.

- The most transferrable skills are those focused on leadership and decision-making, but, even then the nature of the portability of these talents is somewhat dependent on the specific industry or corporate culture.

- If you're looking to bring in a star from outside, think carefully about how well they fit into, and match, your corporate culture and organisational challenges ahead.

- If you consider yourself a high-flier and are keen on making the next big move, consider what made you a high-flier in the first place and if this will be relevant in a potential new role.

What you might say about this

'He might have been a great success at his former firm, but the "portability of talent theory" suggests we shouldn't expect this to be completely replicated here.'

'How much of my current success is dependent on my working environment?'

'I think we should look to promote from within. Hiring from outside is expensive and it's not obvious that it's always successful.'

Where you can find out more

Boris Groysberg, *Chasing Stars: The Myth of Talent and the Portability of Performance*, Princeton University Press, 2010.

'Are leaders portable?', Boris Groysberg, Andrew N. McLean and Nitin Nohria, *Harvard Business Review*, May 2006.

IDEA #68
Do I have a choice?

When people feel they have choice they perceive their workload to be lighter.

What you need to know

An increasingly popular psychological concept known as 'cognitive dissonance' describes when a person undertakes an action that is in conflict with a strongly held belief and subsequently seeks to justify or rationalise their action. In the process, errors of judgement or perception frequently occur.

For example, the researchers Emily Balcetis and David Dunning sought to investigate the impact of cognitive dissonance on spatial perceptions. They divided college students into two groups, both of whom were asked to walk across a campus quad and back (111.2m each way). The students 'were taken outside to a highly trafficked … quad at the centre of campus … [and the] experimenter handed subjects a Carmen Miranda [a Brazilian samba singer famous in 1950s Hollywood] costume, including grass skirt, coconut bra, hat adorned in plastic fruit and flower lei. Students were told to put on the costume, walk the width of the quad alone and return, before answering questions about their emotions and experiences.' Critically, one group of students were told they could decline the request, whereas the other group were given no choice. The researchers wanted to understand what impact the variable of choice had on how far the students estimated the distance they walked.

Amazingly, the students who were given the option of rejecting the costume and task estimated the length of the quad to be around 110–60m less than the estimate given by those who were given no choice.

Why it matters

According to Balcetis and Dunning, the misperception of the quad length is all down to choice: those who had no choice regarding wearing the Carmen Miranda costume seemed to react against the task by perceiving its difficulty (i.e., the distance walked) to be greater than the reality. In a second experiment covered in the paper, similar findings were uncovered where students were asked to push themselves up a hill while kneeling on a skateboard. Those who felt they had chosen to do this estimated the steepness of the hill to be significantly less than those who had no choice. Giving people choice – or the semblance of choice – seems to reduce the perceived difficulty of a task.

How this will change the way you work

- *Offer a choice.* A constant gripe of employees is a lack of ownership of and autonomy in their work; often blamed on overbearing, micro-managing or dictatorial bosses. The evidence from the Carmen Miranda and skateboarding studies suggest that simply by giving individuals the freedom to reject their tasks (which, in most workplaces, they usually will not) leads to a reduction in the perceived onerousness of the work at hand. Whether this benefit lasts for a long time or not remains to be tested, but it's hard to see a downside to offering your team choice in their work every now and again.

What you might say about this

'Team, we've got a series of tasks to do this week – who wants to do what?'

'You don't have to this if you don't want to – someone else can pick it up if need be.'

'I need to make my team feel they have more ownership of their work.'

Where you can find out more

'Cognitive dissonance and the perception of natural environments', Emily Balcetis and David Dunning, *Psychological Science*, Vol. 18, No. 10, 2007.

IDEA #69
What not to write

Long words make people look less, not more, intelligent.

What you need to know

A common trait of student life is to pad out rushed essays with verbose linguistic fluff to meet a set word limit. The belief underpinning this is that longer words make the writer seem more intelligent. Winner of the 2006 Ig Nobel Prize (a parody of the Nobel Prize, specialising in rewarding humorous research), Daniel Oppenheimer of Princeton University, researched the impact of using long words where a shorter one would suffice and demonstrated that, in reality, the opposite is true.

Oppenheimer supported his hypothesis through a variety of experiments. In one experiment, two types of documents (including graduate school applications and sociology and philosophy student essays) were evaluated by participants; one type contained longer words, the other had – where appropriate – shorter ones substituted in. In this experiment, participants judged the writers of the documents with shorter words to be more intelligent than those with longer words. In another experiment Oppenheimer demonstrated that, in foreign text translations, those with shorter words were judged to have come from smarter authors. In a slightly different experiment, Oppenheimer found that monographs written in hard-to-read fonts were perceived to have come from less intelligent authors (although, intriguingly, Oppenheimer has conducted later research that also suggests texts which are hard to read are actually easier to remember). For the 75 per cent or so of students who admit to using longer words to look smarter, this is disappointing news.

Why it matters

The most likely explanation for this counter-intuitive discovery is information that is easy to process (i.e., written in simpler text or font) is equated with being more intelligently written and therefore to have come from the pen of a more intelligent author. Students are not the only group to be criticised for use of purple prose. Business writing – in presentations, reports or public statements – is frequently held up to ridicule for its overuse of jargon. Each year the *Financial Times* columnist Lucy Kellaway metaphorically hands out the Golden Flannel Awards for best business jargon (the most recent winner was the Burberry CEO's annual report statement, which read: 'in the wholesale channel, Burberry exited doors not aligned with brand status and invested in presentation through both enhanced assortments and dedicated, customised real estate in key doors').

While Oppenheimer's research focused on graduate school work, there can be little doubt of its applicability to the world of business' linguistic loquaciousness – or, in simpler terms, jargon.

How this will change the way you work

- *Keep everything as simple and as clear as possible.* Perceived author intelligence correlates with how easy it is for a reader to process one's writing. If you can't make something simple to understand on paper, it might not necessarily be because the problem is too complex to explain. It might instead be that you do not understand the problem well enough to explain it clearly.

What you might say about this

'She talks in long words and it all sounds very complicated. In reality, I think she's hiding the fact she doesn't really understand.'

'If you can't explain something clearly, then you clearly don't understand it well enough.'

'Business jargon makes you look stupid. So does long-winded waffle.'

Where you can find out more

'Consequences of erudite vernacular utilized irrespective of necessity: Problems with using long words needlessly', Daniel M. Oppenheimer, *Applied Cognitive Psychology*, Vol. 20, No. 2, 2005.

'Hard-to-read fonts promote better recall', Daniel M. Oppenheimer, *Harvard Business Review*, March 2012.

IDEA #70
F**k that hurts! How swearing eases the pain

Long a workplace taboo, swearing has unexpected and powerful benefits.

What you need to know

As Steven Pinker, the Harvard University-based psychologist, has pointed out, since religiously inspired expletives such as 'hell', 'damn', and 'Jesus Christ' entered the English lexicon aeons ago, swearing has been socially frowned upon, treated as a sign of aggression or lack of self-discipline. Yet, despite its low standing, it remains as commonplace as ever to hear individuals breach expected social norms by turning the airwaves blue. Pinker, in an entertaining essay in the *New Republic*, has questioned why swearing remains taboo while also demonstrating its powerful impact on triggering heightened emotional recall – swear words (at least for native speakers) affect us in weird, personal and wonderful ways that are little understood. But beyond fascinating neuroscientific findings into how our brains react when people swear, a research team led by Dr Richard Stephens at Keele University has uncovered a surprising positive benefit of cursing: it helps to reduce pain and increase one's ability to withstand it.

In an experiment, 64 volunteers each submerged a hand in freezing water (known as testing for 'cold-pressor pain tolerance') while repeating a profanity of their choice. The volunteers then repeated the experiment, but this time uttering a non-sacred word that they would use to describe a table (e.g., 'surface'). On average, participants could tolerate the icy water for nearly two minutes when they were swearing, compared to only 75 seconds when they were forbidden from uttering expletives. As concluded in the study, swearing appeared to give a 'pain-lessening (hypoalgesic) effect'.

Why it matters

The Keele University finding was unexpected as prior to the study it was commonly assumed that swearing actually makes things worse as it encourages people to 'catastrophise' a problem (i.e., to exaggerate and focus in on it). Dr Stephens suggests that one reason for swearing's pain-reducing effect is that it raises aggression levels in the body, which in turn reduce feelings of pain. Cursing would appear to induce a 'fight-or-flight response' and in the process 'nullifies the link between fear of pain and pain perception'. By distracting our minds from the feeling of pain, swearing would appear to help us refocus on dealing with the problem at hand, rather than wallowing in the pain caused.

How this will change the way you work

- Who is the swearing directed at? In all but the most testosterone-fuelled workplace settings swearing is not considered good practice. However, the research from Keele University suggests a much more sanguine approach could be taken towards swearing in the office – particularly if the swearing is not directed at anyone. Taking out aggression on others is clearly not acceptable, but if it's only internally directed, it may actually be helpful in allowing the swearer to lessen the impact of their suffering. So the next time your computer crashes and wipes out a week's worth of work, feel free to let rip with the profanities – you should feel better.

What you might say about this

'Sh*t – I just stubbed my toe!'

'As long as you don't swear aggressively at colleagues, I'm pretty relaxed about the use of swear words in the workplace.'

'I need to calm down. Excuse my language for a moment ...'

Where you can find out more

'Swearing as a response to pain', R. Stephens, J. Atkins and A. Kingston, *Neuroreport*, Vol. 20, No. 12, 2009.

'What the f***?', Steven Pinker, *The New Republic*, 2007.

IDEA #71
When you should turn that frown upside down

Simply altering your facial expressions can change your feelings and thoughts.

What you need to know

In 1872, the great Charles Darwin wrote that 'the free expression by outward signs of an emotion intensifies it'. In other words, if we look happy and demonstrate it through smiling, we will in turn feel happier. It took nearly 100 years for the idea to gain much attention from psychologists, but since then a great deal of research has built up to show that – even subconsciously – how we appear outwardly in terms of our emotions has an impact on how we think and feel.

Why it matters

Take two of the most common facial expressions: smiling and frowning. In a number of experiments, participants were induced to either smile or frown, with the impact of this tested across several measures. On most occasions the participants were completely unaware that the test had anything to do with emotion or facial expressions – for example, in one experiment individuals were asked to hold a pencil with their lips in a way that forced them to 'fake' a variety of smiles (try it!). The results were unexpected.

- When smiling, participants:
  - o rated cartoon or video clips funnier than non-smiling participants;
  - o made decisions more quickly and intuitively;
  - o were treated more leniently when being punished for academic misconduct.
- When frowning, participants:
  - o felt more pain from an unpleasant procedure on their forearms;
  - o thought more carefully and rationally about tricky decisions;
  - o were less likely to be affected by cognitive biases (such as the better-than-average effect – see Idea #11).

How this will change the way you work

- Furrow your brow … or just smile. The old mantra 'smile, it'll make you feel happier' may well be true – at least in the short term. Equally, frowning could also have value, as it helps to engage the more rational, deliberative and analytical parts of our brain (see Idea #35), which in turn helps us to make better decisions. Obviously you can't spend your life with a fake smile or frown on your face, but every once in a while if you feel your energy levels sapping or want to really concentrate on a tough decision, try engaging your facial muscles.

- As an interesting aside, a study from the University of Cardiff has suggested that happiness levels for people who struggle to frown – such as individuals who have received Botox injections – are, on average, higher than for those with no facial impairments. However, other research has suggested that this may be at the detriment of being able to process the emotional state of others accurately.

What you might say about this

'Feeling down? Smile!'

'He must really be concentrating – he's frowning.'

'You know when an audience is warmed up before a comedy gig? The organisers do it so the audience find the content funnier because they're already smiling by the time the main act comes on.'

Where you can find out more

'Duchenne smile, emotional experience, and automatic reactivity: A test of the facial feedback hypothesis', R. Soussignan, *Emotion*, Vol. 2, No. 1, 2002.

'Overcoming intuition: Metacognitive difficulty activates analytic reasoning', Adam L. Alter, Daniel M. Oppenheimer, Nicholas Epley and Rebecca N. Eyre, *Journal of Experimental Psychology: General*, Vol. 136, No. 4, 2007.

'Feeling and facial efference: Implications of the vascular theory of emotion', Robert B. Zajonc, Sheila T. Murphy and Marita Inglehart, *Psychological Review*, Vol. 96, No. 3, 1989.

IDEA #72
How to become Mr Charismatic, JFK-style

Twelve tactics for becoming more charismatic.

What you need to know

John Antonakis, a professor of organisational behaviour at the University of Lausanne, has led research that has uncovered 12 'charismatic leadership tactics' (CLTs) to help you become a more inspirational leader. Working from the first principle that charisma is a skill which can be learnt, Antonakis has trained business leaders in using CLTs and observed a noticeable jump in the perceived effectiveness of these leaders: in one instance, the leadership ratings of individuals newly trained in CLTs rose by around 60 per cent, as scored by observers.

Why it matters

While the charisma of a leader may not lead to bottom-line performance improvement (see Idea #26), research suggests that people *perceive* charismatic leaders to be more effective than dull ones. According to Antonakis, in eight out of the last ten US presidential elections the winning candidates used more CLTs than their opponents. With this in mind, why wouldn't you want to be a bit more like Barack Obama or Steve Jobs when delivering the next quarterly results presentation?

How this will change the way you work

The 12 CLTs split into verbal and non-verbal groups. They can be used in major presentations or just in everyday workplace interactions. You don't need to use them all in one go (in fact this would probably be a bit distracting for the recipient if you've never used them before), so balance how and when you apply them carefully. Next time you're preparing for a meeting think about how you can drop some of these in.

Verbal CLTs:

- *stories and anecdotes* make you seem more human, e.g., 'Fighting through serious illness helped me appreciate how we need to make sure we spend our time doing things we really believe in';

- *metaphors, similes and analogies* help to make a situation visceral and real, e.g., 'We're on the edge of a fiscal cliff here';

- *rhetorical questions* linger in the memory, e.g., 'Do we want to work at a company that we can be proud of when we look back on our lives?';

- *contrasts* help to sharpen a point by opposing it to something, e.g., 'Ask not what can your team do for you, but what can you do for your team';

- *three point lists* are punchy, logical and give the impression of being comprehensive, e.g., 'This is the right strategy for us because it aligns with our core values, fits in with market conditions and plays to our core competencies';

- *statements of moral conviction* help to show your passions and true character, e.g., 'I would never do anything that would take advantage of people';
- *reflections of group sentiments* can help make you a moral compass for people, e.g., 'We believe in always doing the very best for the taxpayer';
- *setting high goals* makes your vision appear aspirational, e.g., 'We will be the market leader in five years';
- *combining high goals with evidence that you can deliver this* inspires confidence, e.g., 'I made my previous company the best in its field and I'll do the same here'.

Non-verbal CLTs:

- *using your voice* – from whispering to raising the volume to introducing dramatic pauses – helps to convey passion and excitement;
- *using your face* – such as making eye contact, smiling, laughing – helps to back-up your message and make it more memorable;
- *using your body* – hand gestures or even poses – can help elucidate a point.

What you might say about this

'Charisma isn't some innate skill that only a special few have – you can learn it.'

'Next time I prepare a presentation I'm going to include some CLTs.'

'Our analysis is only a part of what will make this presentation great – I need to use some CLTs to really draw out the key messages.'

Where you can find out more

'Learning charisma', John Antonakis, Marika Fenley and Sue Liechti, *Harvard Business Review*, June 2012.

David V. Day and John Antonakis (eds), *The Nature of Leadership:* (2nd edn), Sage Publications, 2012.

IDEA #73
My greatest weakness?
I'm a perfectionist ...

Being honest and candid in an interview will help rather than hinder you.

What you need to know

It's a classic dilemma. There's a world-class firm that you're about to interview for. Its values are doing the best for its clients – code for 'maximising shareholder profit'. You know it will be a terrific career boost if you get a job there, but you also know your own personal values differ quite a bit from the firm's and your current skillset is somewhat different from the skills traditionally expected at the firm. In the interview do you: a) pretend that you were born to work at the firm; or b) be true to yourself and answer candidly about what your real values and skills are?

Research by Daniel M. Cable of London Business School and Virginia S. Kay of the University of North Carolina at Chapel Hill suggests the latter option (called 'choosing to self-verify') wins every time. The academics took a cohort of 146 MBA students and followed their development from their time as MBA students to their first forays into the job market. Capturing data on the students' pre-matriculation interview admissions assessments, final grade point average and several self-assessments (asking questions on a point scale such as, 'It's important for an employer to see me as I see myself, even if it means bringing people to recognise my limitations' and 'I like to be myself rather than trying to act like someone I'm not') over the time period, the study tested an individual's propensity towards self-verification during their careers.

Not only did the researchers find no clear relationship between self-verification and the number of job offers received by candidates (in other words, being honest about your beliefs and skills does not reduce your ability to get a job) they also found several unexpected benefits of being true to yourself.

Why it matters

Based on the MBA student study and a further survey of 208 job-seekers for international teaching positions, the researchers discovered that individuals who self-verified had higher levels of job satisfaction, a greater feeling of commitment to the work they did and better ratings from supervisors. Furthermore, they found that admissions officers at business schools have an easier job of predicting future career performance for those who are more candid about themselves.

Cable and Kay suggest three reasons for why 'self-verifiers' have better job outcomes. First, by being candid about their strengths and weaknesses, self-verifiers 'are more likely to be selected into jobs they can actually perform'. Second, individuals who mask their true personalities can create 'a sense of alienation from oneself which increases emotional exhaustion' and in turn takes up energy that would otherwise have been used on job performance. Third, those who self-verify are more likely to end up working at companies that actually reflect their personal values, which consequently makes for a more fulfilling working experience.

How this will change the way you work

- Be honest about who you are and what you believe in when job-hunting. There's no evidence to suggest that being candid in this way actually decreases your job prospects and a considerable weight of research suggesting the contrary: the more honest you are in your job interviews, the more likely you are to get and enjoy your job.

- If you feel like you need to put on a mask to convince someone you want to work for them, you're at risk of having an unfulfilled and unhappy employment.

What you might say about this

'Be true to yourself – answer the questions honestly and candidly.'

'We want to work with honest people. If you want to work here you need to be truthful in your interviews.'

'My personal values really don't match this company's. So why do I want to work for them? Are these reasons good enough to risk being unhappy in my job?'

Where you can find out more

'Striving for self-verification during organizational entry', Daniel M. Cable and Virginia S. Kay, *Academy of Management Journal*, Vol. 55, No. 2, 2012.

IDEA #74
Start up where you started from

The benefits of 'regional embeddedness'

What you need to know

Michael S. Dahl of Aalborg University and Olav Sorenson of Yale University studied the impact that 'regional embeddedness' – how well you know your local area – has on the success of entrepreneurial start-ups. Analysing data on more than 13,000 Danish start-up businesses, Dahl and Sorenson were able to demonstrate that 'regional embeddedness' gives greater benefit to entrepreneurs than prior industry knowledge – a well-known source of competitive advantage. After controlling for education, background and other demographic factors, the academics calculated that 'relative to a newcomer [to a regional area], an entrepreneur with [previous] tenure in a region (on average 6.4 years) has a 9 per cent lower exit rate and earns roughly $8,172 more in annual profits'. By comparison, 'relative to a *de novo* entrant, an entrepreneur with [previous] experience in the industry ... has an 11 per cent lower rate of exit and earns $3,508 more in annual profits'.

Why it matters

Dahl and Sorenson started from the premise that while many entrepreneurs choose to start up businesses near to where they live, a commonly cited reason for this is to be close their family and friends. Consequently, the researchers wanted to test whether this proximity to loved ones actually causes a distraction to budding entrepreneurs that harms their bottom-line returns. Conversely, some entrepreneurs take the opposite view and are keen to try their skills in a 'new region' to get away from their pasts. In both instances, the researchers got clear answers. Knowing your area – even if you didn't necessarily work there before – can make a significant positive impact on the outcome of your business and being close to friends and family appears to have no negative or distracting effects on one's entrepreneurial success.

How this will change the way you work

- *Success begins near home.* If you're of an entrepreneurial disposition and age (research has shown that the peak age for an individual to start up a successful business, with success defined in terms of a start-up's longevity, is 42 years old) the advice is clear: if you want to give yourself the best chance of success, in the first instance at least, start with what you know and where you know.

What you might say about this

'I know it seems exciting starting in a new region, but I really think it's unwise – you're better off starting with an area you know well and then expanding.'

'Think more broadly about what your competitive advantages are – if you know a region really well, that's a potential source of positive distinction.'

'It's a double bonus. I know this place like the back of my hand and I get to be closer to the family.'

Where you can find out more

'Home sweet home: Entrepreneurs' location choices and the performance of their ventures', Michael S. Dahl and Olav Sorenson, *Management Science*, Vol. 58, No. 6, 2012.

'Are you experienced? Prior experience and the survival of new organizations', Michael S. Dahl and Toke Reichstein, *Industry and Innovation*, Vol. 14, No. 5, 2007.

IDEA #75
How to expand time

You can increase the time you have by giving some of it up in the aid of others.

What you need to know

Through a number of innovative experiments, Cassie Mogilner of the Wharton School led a team of researchers to uncover what happens to people's subjective sense of 'time affluence' (in other words, how much time they believe they have) when they use their time to help others. In one experiment, two groups could either spend five minutes writing a letter to a gravely ill child or five minutes counting the number of letter 'e's in a Latin text. In another test, one group were assigned time to help someone of their choice, while the rest could leave the session early, and in another experiment groups either spent 15 minutes helping edit the research essay of an 'at-risk' (i.e., disadvantaged) student from a local state school or were given free time to spend on themselves.

In each experiment, the conclusion was clear: giving time to others made individuals feel 'more "time affluent" and less time-constrained' – even compared to those people who had been given free time to use as they pleased. Specifically, those who gave time in aid of others compared to those who did not, when asked, were: a) more likely to say they felt their futures were 'infinite'; b) more likely to commit greater amounts of time to a given task the following week; and c) felt they made more effective use of their time.

Why it matters

For many people, time is more precious than money. You can't buy it. You can't sell it. You can't make more of it – or can you? Mogilner *et al.*'s work suggests that, while clearly you can't *objectively* increase time, *subjectively* you can. Chiming with research that suggests people who give away their money feel richer as a result, spending your time in the aid of others can make you feel more time-rich.

How this will change the way you work

- *Give a little, get a lot.* Somewhat surprisingly, it seemed that the amount of time people spent on others did not make an impact on increased feelings of 'time affluence'. In the experiment where participants wrote a letter to an ill child, some individuals were asked to spend 30 minutes on the task while others spent only ten minutes. Yet both sets of individuals responded with similar conviction that they felt their future time was 'infinite' following the experiment. Consequently, it seems that even giving just a little time to help others can go a long way to making you feel that you have more time for yourself.

- *Make the time.* On a personal basis, you should seek opportunities to put this research into practice by setting aside small amounts of time to help others – even if it is just a helpful call or email to a colleague. Organisations, on the other hand, could look to formalise processes whereby employees give something back to the community, through pro bono initiatives, for instance. Feeling that there is not enough time in the day to complete your work leads to great pressure and strain. If something so simple as helping others for a little while can both reduce this strain and make you feel more effective (and, as a result, make you more likely to be more productive), it seems like an obvious choice to give up a bit of your time to help those in need.

What you might say about this

'I'm feeling completely swamped – I don't have time to help others, let alone myself – but maybe I should give this a try.'

'We spend so much time procrastinating through checking emails or surfing the Web yet we rarely feel much better afterwards – helping others might be a simple way to change this.'

'I'm not going to watch television tonight to unwind. I'm going to call a friend in need and see if I can help in any way instead.'

Where you can find out more

'Giving time gives you time', Cassie Mogilner, Zoë Chance and Michael I. Norton, *Psychological Science*, September 2012.

'You'll feel less rushed if you give time away', Cassie Mogilner, *Harvard Business Review*, September 2012.

IDEA #76
Let's *not* pull an all-nighter

In impairment terms, averaging four to five hours of sleep a night is equivalent to having a blood alcohol level of 0.1 per cent – the same as downing four bottles of beer.

What you need to know

Michael Christian of the University of North Carolina and Aleksander Ellis of the University of Arizona have demonstrated that not only does sleep deprivation lead to poor performance on any task that requires 'innovative thinking, risk analysis and strategic planning' but it also leads to more unethical behaviour in the workplace. Using research on nurses at a large medical centre and undergraduate students participating in a lab study, Christian and Ellis' work has demonstrated that a lack of sleep can lead individuals to be ruder than usual and, worryingly, to attempt to take more money than they are owed. The researchers suggest that this deviant behaviour is due to a lack of glucose production caused by sleep deprivation. The prefrontal cortex area – the part of the brain that governs cognitive behaviour and decision-making (known as the 'executive functions') – does not receive enough glucose and, as a result, erratic and irrational behaviour ensues.

Why it matters

As Charles A. Czeisler of Harvard Medical School has argued, a blood alcohol level of 0.10 per cent is equivalent to a man weighing around 80 kilograms drinking four bottles of beer. Nobody in their right mind would encourage you to go about your daily work routine having just downed four beers. Yet this is in effect what happens when managers encourage their team members to burn the midnight oil. We often romanticise or even glorify such hard-working behaviour as being 'all part of the job' in high-pressure industries, but this may be extremely faulty logic. According to research by the National Sleep Disorders Research Plan – cited by Christian and Ellis – sleep deprivation costs the US economy $150 billion per annum through accidents and lost productivity. Factoring in the statistic that between the end of 1999 and 2009 the number of Americans sleeping less than six hours a night increased from 13 per cent to 20 per cent gives cause for concern.

How this will change the way you work

- *Enforce down-time.* Czeisler is emphatic that employers need to have greater concern for the sleep patterns of their workers. For example, he recommends that 'a company's sleep policy should not permit anyone, under any circumstances, to take an overnight flight and then to drive to a business meeting.' Similarly, he believes that employers should not encourage scheduled work beyond 16 hours a day.

- *Recognise the dangers of insufficient sleep.* It seems unbelievable the extent to which long working hours are part of some industries' cultures. Junior doctors in many countries are still forced to work back-to-back night and day shifts – despite evidence showing that hospital interns are 61 per cent more likely to stab themselves with a needle or scalpel following 24 consecutive hours of work. Not only do employers put their employees' health at risk by encouraging this behaviour but they also put the performance of the firm – or even the safety of their customers – in danger, too.

What you might say about this

'Sleep deprivation can cause health, immunological and memory retention issues – it's a serious problem.'

'Let's record the number of hours people work and intervene where necessary to reduce their workloads.'

'I don't see treating sleep deprivation seriously as being "nice" to our employees – it's just common sense. If they don't have enough sleep, they'll perform poorly and the company will suffer.'

Where you can find out more

'Sleep deficit: The performance killer, a conversation with Harvard Medical School Professor Charles A. Czeisler', Charles A. Czeisler and Bronwyn Fryer, Harvard Business Review, October 2006.

'Examining the effects of sleep deprivation on workplace deviance: A self-regulatory perspective', Michael S. Christian and Aleksander P.J. Ellis, Academy of Management Journal, Vol. 54, No. 5, 2011.

IDEA #77
Keeping out the fifth column

How to keep your organisation's trade secrets under wraps.

What you need to know

In 2002, the American Society for Industrial Security surveyed over 130 firms and reported that more than 40 per cent had experienced actual or presumed losses of 'trade secrets' in the preceding year. In financial terms, it was estimated that the companies represented by the survey – Fortune 1000 companies and SMEs – would have made a whopping loss of more than $50 billion from exposed trade secrets or intellectual property theft.

David Hannah, of the Beedie School of Business at Simon Fraser University, sought to find out how companies could prevent these trade secret losses through an in-depth analysis of the operating patterns of a small-sized US technology company (125 employees) and a large global technology firm (more than 70,000 employees). To start with, Hannah had to define what we mean by 'trade secrets', which are just one part of intellectual property. In the US, a trade secret must conform to three legal requirements: a) it must contain information – for example, a formula (such as the Kentucky Fried Chicken recipe) or process; b) it must be valuable to the owning organisation and in part its value must be derived from the exclusivity the owning organisation has over it; and c) it must be apparent that the organisation claiming ownership of the trade secret has made efforts to keep it secret.

Why it matters

Through clearly defining what the term means and analysing what worked and what didn't in his organisational case studies, Hannah was able to clear up one popular myth straight away: trade secrets are not (in the overwhelming amount of cases) stolen from competitors through Bond-like espionage. They leak out from a combination of unknowingly ignorant or disgruntled current or former employees. So the burden rests on management to make sure these individuals – and trade secret policies – are appropriately managed.

How this will change the way you work

Hannah identified four pieces of advice that can help organisations to protect their prized secrets.

- *Don't inform employees of trade secret policies during inductions.* Company policy regarding trade secret disclosures are invariably bundled into a ream of disclosure agreements, health and safety policy, IT security policies, etc. that new employees have to sign on joining a company. Employees are thus subjected to information overload, and may struggle to remember what they signed, let alone what they were told. Companies should stagger what policies are signed when and ensure that employees are frequently reminded of their responsibilities.

- *Differentiate between handling procedures and access restrictions.* Research has shown that if employees do not feel trusted they are more likely to divulge – unwittingly or not – trade secrets. In practice, trust can often be inferred by individuals on the basis of whether they have been subjected to access restrictions (e.g., they are forbidden from accessing certain files) or handling procedures (e.g., they are briefed on the importance of not sharing information that they do have access to). In the case of the former, employees believe they are not trusted, in the case of the latter they believe they are. Where possible try to err on the side of enforcing handling procedures. If you need to impose access restrictions, make sure the employees are aware of why these exist and highlight the materials they do have access to – this will help make them feel more trusted.

- *Clarify who owns what.* Many employees believe that they own the rights to work they undertake while in the office. Whether they've come up with a new idea or business model, if an employee has signed an assignment provision, the idea belongs to their employer – not to them.

- *Manage exits carefully.* Even after leaving a company, former employees retain a legal responsibility to protect the trade secrets of their erstwhile paymasters. Exit interviews should gently remind individuals of this. Where partings are on less than friendly terms, organisations would be wise to ensure their legal department send out a formal reminder of the ongoing trade secret requirements former employees are still subject to.

What you might say about this

'We're granting you access to this privileged information because we trust that you won't share it.'

'Every quarter we should remind all employees of our trade secrets policy.'

'I'm nervous about him leaving. We should make sure the legal department reminds him of his responsibilities towards us and the repercussions of breaching these.'

Where you can find out more

'Keeping trade secrets secret', David R. Hannah, *MIT Sloan Management Review*, No. 47, Spring 2006.

IDEA #78
How to pick your next leader

What a leader's background says about their potential success.

What you need to know

Through an historical analysis of hundreds of business, military and political leaders, Gautam Mukunda of Harvard Business School, has developed a theory to explain how and why some leaders make a greater impact on history than others, but on the whole, most leaders make relatively little difference to the organisations they lead. According to Mukunda, leaders are 'filtered' by three factors and the extent to which leaders are filtered determines how likely they are to make an indelible mark on history. The three elements of Mukunda's 'Leadership Filtration Theory' are:

- *external operating environment* – such as the state of economy or wars

- *dynamics within organisations* – such as the extent to which leaders are hamstrung by bureaucracy

- *leadership selection* – the way most leaders are selected tends to generate indentikit candidates who perpetuate prevailing norms.

To give examples of what 'unfiltered' or 'filtered' leaders look like in practice, John F. Kennedy is rated as a 'filtered' leader, because he had substantial experience in the House and Senate prior to the presidency; by contrast George W. Bush was 'unfiltered' because he had only served six years as a governor prior to becoming president – thus having relatively little experience.

Why it matters

- In Mukunda's diagnosis, the extreme performance of leaders – either very high or very low impact – is largely determined by how 'unfiltered' a leader is. While filtered leaders can have high impact – such as Bill Clinton – most of the time they just provide a steady pair of hands.
- By contrast, unfiltered leaders such as Abraham Lincoln or Winston Churchill, by virtue of being relative outsiders, are more likely to be prepared to shake up the system and try to instigate major change.

How this will change the way you work

- Mukunda's research suggests that while organisations wishing to undertake radical change may look to an unfiltered leader, they should do so with caution. Unfiltered leaders are more liable to result in extremely poor performance and they are harder to evaluate in terms of fitness for office.
- His advice to organisations considering an unfiltered leader is to be smart in matching a candidate's skills to the specific context of their potential leadership (e.g., tough economic times or bright growth prospects); not to dismiss the candidate's statements about their beliefs prior to selection as pure rhetoric, as they may well be more genuine than those of a filtered candidate; and to try and pick a leader who was successfully filtered in other settings and will therefore be more likely to understand how to adapt to bureaucratic necessities.

What you might say about this

'He knows the system inside out – he should provide steady leadership during these difficult times.'

'If we're looking for a radical visionary then we need to look outside our comfort zone for candidates.'

'She sounds like a very exciting candidate, but we need to understand that we're taking a real risk here because we don't really know very much about her.'

Where you can find out more

Gautam Mukunda, *Indispensable: When Leaders Really Matter*, Harvard Business Review Press, 2012.

IDEA #79
Repetition, repetition, repetition

Want your team to make faster progress? Keep nagging them.

What you need to know

How do you get people to do the things you ask of them? Researchers from Harvard Business School and Northwestern University posed this question, focusing on the communication strategies of six project managers operating across three industries. The researchers' study made three startling discoveries:

1. Managers who used 'redundant communication' – repeating the same message over and over again to team members – were more likely to progress actions in their projects quicker than managers who did not.

2. There are communication differences between managers who have direct authority (i.e., line management responsibilities) and those who do not. The latter group make great efforts to communicate messages to employees, often using multiple media platforms (e.g., email, text message, face-to-face communication) to do so, and usually send their messages via different mechanisms in quick succession. By comparison, the former group are more likely to delay communication, often only using emails to make requests. Interestingly, managers without

direct authority are usually more effective at managing their team members' tasks as a consequence.

3. When communicating with employees, it appears that the clarity of the message (i.e., stating clearly what needs to be done) matters much less than the volume of messages and the number of times each message is delivered.

Why it matters

Do you ever worry that you are being a bore or a pain at work? That you're constantly asking for the same request over and over again? Well, you should stop worrying. The findings from this research suggest that if you really want to get things done, you need to bug people until they happen. Just because you once made a request nicely and clearly does not necessarily mean you will actually be delivered what you need.

How this will change the way you work

The key here is to have a sensible strategy when making requests of people. Who are you asking something of and why? Are you their manager or not?

- If you do manage them, you should not assume they will complete your request by simple virtue of hierarchy – you need to monitor the request and make sure they deliver.

- If you do not manage them, the best course of action might be to use redundant communication to make sure the request is clearly stated across multiple channels – that way there can be no doubt about what is requested and its urgency.

What you might say about this

'I'm glad we could talk about this face-to-face but I'll follow up the request with an email.'

'It's really critical that this piece of work gets done on time. It won't harm things if I just send a quick reminder email about its importance.'

'Don't worry about constantly following up requests. It's a sensible strategy for getting stuff done.'

Where you can find out more

'How managers use multiple media: Discrepant events, power, and timing in redundant communication', Paul M. Leonardi, Tsedal B. Neeley and Elizabeth M. Gerber, *Organization Science*, Vol. 23, No. 1, 2012.

IDEA #80
Strike a pose, feel the power

Simply adjusting the way we stand or sit can have an important biological and psychological effect on how powerful we feel.

What you need to know

Researchers from Columbia University and Harvard University ran an experiment where male and female participants were asked to adopt four different poses for one minute each. The poses comprised two 'high-power' body positions (sat in a chair, arms behind head and feet up on desk; and standing upright behind a table, legs apart, hands resting weight on the table and leaning forward) and two 'low-power' body positions (sat in a chair, feet firmly on the floor, hands on lap and elbows tucked inside the chair armrests; and standing upright, legs close together and arms folded across each other, as if the participants were trying to hug themselves). After the pose-holding minute, participants were first given $2 and then asked if they would take a 50:50 $2 gamble to double their money. Second, they were asked to rate how 'powerful' and 'in charge' they felt on a scale of 1 (not at all) to 4 (a lot).

Saliva tests were also taken before and after the experiment. The aim of the experiment was to find out whether simply adopting a 'power pose' would increase an individual's risk-taking appetite and their feelings of power, as well as to examine whether any biological changes would take place as a result of the poses. In particular, the academics were keen to discover whether testosterone (a hormone commonly associated with feelings of power) and cortisol (a hormone often taken as a proxy for feelings of stress) would change as a result of the poses. To avoid any unwanted behaviour that might bias the results, participants were told the study was regarding research into changes in heart rate in different scenarios – and all were hooked up to electrocardiography (ECG) monitors.

Why it matters

The researchers' hypotheses were confirmed on all counts. Of the participants who had adopted 'high-power' body positions, 86 per cent gambled their $2 in pursuit of $4 (a risky, but nonetheless reasonably rational choice) whereas a much lower 60 per cent of 'low-power' posers chose to take the gamble. 'High-power' posers reported feelings of power on a scale of 1 to 4 at an average of 2.57 compared with 1.83 for 'low-power' posers. Most fascinatingly, 'high-power' posers' testosterone levels rose relative to baseline by 19 per cent while cortisol levels dropped by 25 per cent, whereas 'low-power' posers' testosterone levels declined by 10 per cent and cortisol levels rose as a result of the body positions by 17 per cent.

No significant gender differences were noticed in the main findings of the study (although, unsurprisingly, testosterone levels were higher at all times in men than women). In short, simply by adopting a more affirmative body pose for a short space of time you can feel more powerful and in control, be more willing to take a risk and change your testosterone and cortisol levels.

How this will change the way you work

- *Check out the poses.* Next time you walk into your office, take a look around and check out how people compose themselves physically. Who is leaning over whom as they talk? Who is hunched up in their chair? Simply adopting 'power poses' might help individuals with low self-esteem or those who feel under pressure or lacking in power.

- *Don't get high on a power trip.* Organisations should take care not to create environments where power poses are the norm – particularly in industries already susceptible to risk-taking. An important consideration to remember is that while power posing may make *you* feel better, it doesn't necessarily mean others will, too.

- *Try to avoid alienating people.* Amy Cuddy, one of the authors of the research into 'power posing' has elsewhere suggested that we commonly make snap judgements of people based on two simple criteria: how likeable they are and how competent they are. 'Power posing' might help on the competence dimension, but it's unlikely to engender feelings of warmth towards anyone.

What you might say about this

'I'm not feeling too great about this interview, but I know that if I sit in a wide "open" posture – taking up a reasonable amount of space – I'll feel more confident.'

'Look how he's sitting – he's clearly trying to make a statement either to himself or others about how powerful he is. It looks ridiculous.'

'Even if you don't feel confident, fake it. Look confident and your hormones will do the rest.'

Where you can find out more

'Power posing: Brief nonverbal displays affect neuroendocrine levels and risk tolerance', Dana R. Carney, Amy J. C. Cuddy and Andy J. Yap, *Psychological Science*, Vol. 21, No. 10, 2010.

'Beliefs about the nonverbal expression of social power', Dana R. Carney, Judith A. Hall and Lavonia Smith LeBeau, *Journal of Nonverbal Behavior*, Vol. 29, No. 2, 2005.

'Just because *I'm nice*, don't assume *I'm dumb*', Amy J.C. Cuddy, *Harvard Business Review*, February 2009.

IDEA #81
Progress – the most important motivator of all

The strongest driver of job happiness is when an employee feels as if progress is being made.

What you need to know

Teresa Amabile, a professor of business administration at Harvard University, and Steven Kramer, a psychologist, undertook a decade-long research project into what makes people tick in the workplace. Covering 238 individuals across 26 projects, seven companies and three industries, the core of Amabile and Kramer's research focused on more than 12,000 work diary entries and daily rankings of individuals' emotional and motivational levels. Expecting to find manager recognition – which, unsurprisingly, managers often think is the key to employee happiness – high on the list of what motivates workers, recognition was in fact conspicuous by its absence. More so than any other factor, *progress* was found to be the greatest driver of workplace satisfaction. Analysing the diary entries, Amabile and Kramer found that on days when employees were happiest, progress was the most frequently reported type of event (76 per cent of the time), compared with team collaboration (53 per cent), instrumental support (43 per cent), interpersonal support (25 per cent) and doing important work (just 19 per cent).

Why it matters

Strategy gurus insist that happy workplaces are ones where 'big, hairy, audacious goals' (to use Jim Collins' term) are set by the organisational leadership team and the rest of the company join together in harmonious pursuit of them. Many will be familiar with the tale about JFK and the janitor who was putting a 'man on the moon'. The message is, together, we achieve great things, but what if striving for great things doesn't actually make for happy or productive workplaces? According to Amabile and Kramer's research, 'doing important work' only featured in diary entries on days ranked as highly fulfilling a fifth of the time. This research provides a timely corrective to the claims that we need to set big goals and happiness will follow suit. Instead, incremental gains, where progress (potentially, though not necessarily, towards a great strategic vision) can actually be felt by the people doing the work is what really makes for a truly engaged and motivated team.

How this will change the way you work

Amabile and Kramer break down how to achieve 'inner work life satisfaction' (in other words, happiness in the workplace) for either yourself or your team into three areas for action:

1. *Create a sense of progress.* Set small, incremental goals that are realistic and timely and celebrate them when they are met. Don't underestimate the power of 'quick wins' in achieving this. If you see something that you can change immediately without resorting to endless bureaucracy, just do it.

2. *Catalyse the project environment and give support to individuals throughout projects.* Examples of this include giving choice (see Idea #68), providing adequate resources and training to people and helping set clear goals.

3. *Provide emotional nourishment.* Keep a keen eye on the interpersonal side of things. Ensure that all team members feel properly respected and supported both by you and their peers. Holding fun team events can help to this end.

What you might say about this

'I'm happy if I feel like I'm achieving something.'

'This is a ten-year strategy. We need to give people clear signals that they're on track towards this so we can build a sense of progress and momentum.'

'In terms of workplace satisfaction, people don't care that much about what their bosses think – they care much more about how they feel themselves.'

Where you can find out more

Teresa M. Amabile and Steven J. Kramer, *The Progress Principle: Using Small Wins to Ignite Joy, Engagement, and Creativity at Work*, Harvard Business Review Press, 2011.

'What really motivates workers', Teresa M. Amabile and Steven J. Kramer, *Harvard Business Review*, January 2010.

IDEA #82
Elbow grease – the value generator

We ascribe greater value to items we have helped create than ones we haven't.

What you need to know

Beyond offering good value and stylish design, are there other factors at play in explaining the global success of the Swedish self-assembly furniture giant IKEA? According to research coming from Harvard Business School, the extent to which we are involved in the creation of our IKEA furniture or other products helps to raise the value of the item in our eyes. Building on the 'effort justification' thesis espoused by Matthew White and Paul Dolan (which explains the paradox that for many people work is both their 'most rewarding *and* least pleasurable' activity), Michael Norton, Daniel Mochon and Dan Ariely conducted four experiments to shed light on the 'IKEA effect'.

In the first experiment a selection of participants were asked to assemble an IKEA storage box whereas others were merely tasked with inspecting the boxes. When offered the opportunity to purchase the boxes, the assemblers offered 63 per cent more than the inspectors for the identical box. In the second experiment individuals were told to build an origami figure, then asked to value their creations. Compared with individuals who also valued the origami creations but had not made them, the crafters put a value on their creations at nearly five times the amount of non-crafters. In a third experiment, participants were shown to value Lego sets they had created more highly than ones others had created. In a fourth experiment, it was demonstrated that if participants did not complete the assembly of the IKEA storage box from the first experiment, they valued the product less than participants who had completed the box.

To summarise, the researchers' experiments indicate that if you create an item from start to finish you are more likely to ascribe a significantly greater value to it than if the item was pre-assembled.

Why it matters

How we derive value from goods and services that we purchase is a crucial question any entrepreneur or leader must ask. What makes my product special? What makes people desire it? The 'IKEA effect' suggests that rather than making products fancier, adding the latest technological gizmo or upgrading to a more chic design, value can actually be gained in a much simpler fashion: by making goods and services more interactive and collaborative. While Norton et al.'s experiments only focused on reasonably simple items – a storage box, an origami design – it is worth questioning whether the 'IKEA effect' can be translated to much more complex goods.

How this will change the way you work

- *Engage your customers.* How can you make what you do as interactive as possible with your end-consumers? If you offer consulting services, what can you do to make sure all solutions are co-delivered? If you sell clothes online, how can you make your customers feel like their final purchase has been tailor-made and that they have been involved in its design? Perhaps you could sell 'outfits' that the online shoppers select themselves. Maybe you need to rethink the way your restaurant serves food? Would diners value their meals more if they were involved in its cooking? There are no clear answers to these questions yet, but the 'IKEA effect' should encourage you to think more creatively about how to engage your target markets. If customers feel like they're involved in the design of the product they purchase, they may value it more.

What you might say about this

'The "IKEA effect" explains why he hangs up those awful drawings of his on the wall.'

'It makes complete sense – objectively I know my coffee table is pretty ugly, but I feel an affinity with it because I helped create it.'

'How can we make our business model more like IKEA's in terms of customer engagement with the final product?'

Where you can find out more

'The IKEA effect: When labor leads to love', Michael I. Norton, Daniel Mochon and Dan Ariely, *Journal of Consumer Psychology*, Vol. 22, No. 3, 2012.

'Accounting for the richness of daily activities', Matthew White and Paul Dolan, *Psychological Science*, Vol. 20, No. 8, 2009.

IDEA #83
Getting creative? Get distracted

Our most creative ideas come when we are distracted.

What you need to know

Ap Dijksterhuis and Teun Meurs of the University of Amsterdam sought to explore the impact of 'incubation' – defined as 'the stage during which one refrains from conscious thought and during which the unconscious is at work' – on creativity. The researchers ran three experiments to this end. In each experiment they grouped participants into three different conditions: a) where immediate responses were demanded to the questions posed in the experiments (called the 'immediate condition' and treated as the baseline); b) where participants were encouraged to consciously consider the questions posed for a set amount of time before answering ('conscious thought' condition); and c) where participants were distracted for a set amount of time before answering the questions asked ('unconscious thought' condition).

The results from the experiments clearly showed that participants under the 'unconscious thought' condition came up with answers that were 'more creative … unusual … [and] inaccessible' than participants under the 'conscious thought' condition.

Why it matters

Creativity – along with innovation – has become the Holy Grail for many industries, with business leaders convinced that creativity is the key to unlocking financial growth. However, too often 'creative brainstorming' sessions result in a small minority of vocal individuals barking their long-held thoughts and prejudices at others, with the outputs of the session pitifully labelled as innovative and exciting new thoughts. In reality, the University of Amsterdam research shows that we are at our most creative *not* when we are coerced into thinking consciously about a specific topic and then asked to come up with an answer (the classic brainstorming session). Rather, we are most creative when we are distracted and our ideas are made without too much thought.

How this will change the way you work

- *Don't get stressed.* When thinking up creative ideas, try not to put too much pressure on yourself or others to stay focused on a particular topic. Feel free to let your mind wander before returning to the question at hand.

- *Try the random word game.* An exercise to help do this involves random word association. Generate ideas in a group through a facilitator selecting a specific topic, then add random words into the mix for consideration. For example, you might be concerned with the question, 'how do we increase sales volumes of an IT software package?' The facilitator would then throw in a random word – say, 'duck' – and the rest of the group has to come up with an idea related to this immediately. One idea might be based on the following logic: 'Ducks migrate to more appropriate climates en masse. We need to make our software the obvious choice for consumers (better climate) and also help spread this idea through software-user networks (en masse).' Try it out.

What you might say about this

'We've got a specific problem but we're stuck on it. Let's get creative – get out a book and we'll select a word at random and come up with ideas inspired by that.'

'Don't think too hard about the problem. Our best ideas often come when we least suspect it – often when we're thinking about something else.'

'Sitting in dull rooms, in suits, reading a huge deck of PowerPoint slides is completely contrary to creative thinking. Let's get outside and find inspiration from lots of sources, then come back to the problem. Don't get focused, get distracted.'

Where you can find out more

'Where creativity resides: The generative power of unconscious thought', Ap Dijksterhuis and Teun Meurs, *Consciousness and Cognition*, Vol. 15, No. 1, 2006.

IDEA #84
Avoid the planning fallacy

How long do you think it will take you to read this chapter?

What you need to know

In one of the earliest attempts to quantify the phenomenon known as the 'planning fallacy' – a term coined by the behavioural economists Daniel Kahneman and Amos Tversky – undergraduate psychology students were asked how long it would take them to complete their honours theses. The mean estimate for completion time was 33.9 days, yet the eventual average completion time was 55.5 days. In fact, only 30 per cent of students finished their theses in their estimated time. Since this 1994 study, a wealth of further experiments have comprehensively shown the seemingly ubiquitous failing of humans to accurately assess how long a given task will take. From Canadian taxpayers to Japanese students to industrial

R&D projects, studies from any number of settings have shown that we consistently overestimate our ability to get things done quickly.

Why it matters

Time is money, as the old mantra goes. Yet we are not, it seems, very good at assessing time. Two hypotheses have been advanced for why we succumb to the 'planning fallacy'. The first is something called the 'inside–outside' view. This posits that when we estimate how long something will take to complete, we invariably predict the duration of the task in isolation from other factors which may affect its completion. For instance, it might take a team five working days to complete a report on customer attitudes to a given product range *if* they have fully protected time to undertake the work, with no distractions. Couple the task with 'outside' factors such as competing project commitments, annual leave, sick leave and so forth and the five days could easily stretch into ten. The initial prediction was wrong because it was based on an 'inside' view of the task – it assumed nothing else was going on in the world outside.

A second suggested reason for the 'planning fallacy' is the very nature of planning encourages us to look to the future – and this in turn makes it harder for us to refer back to the past, which is invariably filled with tasks that took us much longer to complete than we originally predicted. Because we are so focused on the future, we neglect this vital historical information.

How this will change the way you work

- *Estimate your error rate.* Before you next have to give an estimate of the likely timescale of anything – from a major strategy overhaul to finishing a report – make sure you have conducted a thorough analysis of your own personal 'planning fallacy' error rate. Make a list of a number of tasks you have to complete and estimate how long it will take you to do so. Then, track the actual time taken to complete and compare it with your estimate to get your error rate. Now, the next time you're asked to predict a timescale, go with your gut instinct, then add on your error rate. Processes like these are used in industries such as construction, where an 'optimism bias' percentage uplift is frequently applied to estimated timescales to account for 'planning fallacy'.

What you might say about this

'That's way too optimistic a deadline. You're falling foul of the "'planning fallacy".'

'What's your planning error rate?'

'Remember the bridge that was over budget and two years late? Another victim of the "planning fallacy".'

Where you can find out more

'Intuitive prediction: Biases and corrective procedures', Daniel Kahneman and Amos Tvserky, *TIMS Studies in the Management Sciences*, Vol. 12, 1979.

'Exploring the 'planning fallacy': Why people underestimate their task completion times', Roger Buehler, Dale Griffin and Michael Ross, *Journal of Personality and Social Psychology*, Vol. 67, No. 3, 1994.

'The planning fallacy: Cognitive, motivational, and social origins', Roger Buehler, Dale Griffin and Johanna Peetz, *Advances in Experimental Social Psychology*, Vol. 43, No. 9, 2010.

IDEA #85
I think the question you're trying to ask is …

When evading the question gives the best answer.

What you need to know

How frustrating is it when politicians or business leaders are asked a specific question but seem to answer another? According to research by Todd Rogers and Michael Norton of Harvard Business School, it's not that annoying for the listener at all. In four different studies covering mock political debates, Norton and Rogers found that 'dodge detection' – a listener's ability to recognise when a speaker has evaded the question posed – is generally quite hard to achieve. They hypothesise that 'dodges go undetected because listeners' attention is not usually directed towards a goal of dodge detection (i.e., is this person answering the question?) but rather a goal of social evaluation (i.e., do I like this person?)'. Their research did acknowledge that when listeners are encouraged to acutely listen out for evasions or when the question answered is substantively different from the one posed, then a listener can more easily detect a dodge, but, intriguingly, it seems answering the wrong question fluently and cogently plays better to an audience than answering the right question poorly.

Why it matters

As the authors of the paper humorously remind the reader, Robert McNamara once famously said, 'don't answer the question you were asked. Answer the question you wish you were asked.' All the time we are posed difficult questions, from 'why haven't I been promoted?' to 'why has the product failed to deliver its promised returns?' From a moral point of view, there is a school of thought that dictates you should answer honestly and truthfully every question asked of you, but, in practice, Norton and Rogers' research suggests, most of the time, conversations are so fast-paced it is actually very hard for the listener to keep track of the original question in the first place. Bearing this in mind, you might consider it expedient to answer your preferred question rather than the one actually asked and take heed of McNamara's counsel.

How this will change the way you work

There are three important implications of this research:

1. *Prepare.* When expecting difficult questions, always prepare answers for them thoroughly in advance. Listeners largely assess the quality of an answer on the fluency of its delivery – sadly the content is often a secondary concern – and so you should always put yourself in a position to achieve this.

2. *Restate.* If you are posed a difficult question that you can't readily answer, every once in a while, it may be the best option – at least

from a presentational point of view – to restate the question in a way that allows you to give an answer you can deliver.

3. *Highlight the evasion.* Taking the opposite angle, if you find yourself in a debate against a speaker who is being frequently evasive when answering questions, don't assume the rest of the audience is able to pick up on this, too. Pointing out to listeners that the speaker is in fact 'dodging' the question will help draw their attention to this and could well act in your favour.

What you might say about this

'That's a very good and complicated question. Let me rephrase it before I answer just so I can make sure I understand ...'

'I know my peer in this discussion sounds very fluent, but if you actually listen to what he's saying, at no point is he actually answering the question posed.'

'A good answer doesn't always have to answer the question asked.'

Where you can find out more

'The artful dodger: Answering the wrong question the right way', Todd Rogers and Michael I. Norton, *Journal of Experimental Psychology: Applied*, Vol. 17, No. 2, 2011.

Part 3

IDEAS ABOUT ORGANI- SATIONS

IDEA #86
Why playing the game will get you ahead

How gaming can revolutionise your workplace.

What you need to know

Games are meant to be fun. Work, by contrast, is only intermittently – if ever – fun. So what would you say if you could make your business more engaging, have more committed employees and more devoted customers – all by making work more fun and, ultimately, more like a game? This is the theory behind 'gamification', a term gaining popularity in a diverse array of industries. Although still rather catholic in its definition, the theory broadly states that the basic principles of gaming – defined by the game designer Jane McGonigal as being a clear goal, rules of engagement, performance feedback and willing participants – can be applied to most business settings and achieve real bottom-line improvements in company performance.

Why it matters

In *For the Win*, by two associate professors from the Wharton School, an internal competition at Microsoft is recounted where employees were encouraged to find translation mistakes in its Windows operating system. Points were awarded for mistakes uncovered and a leaderboard tracked the best performers in the company, providing a competitive edge. Participation was high, with one office even taking an entire day off to dedicate itself to the hunt. The prospect of making work 'fun' has led numerous other organisations to try and adopt gamification techniques in a wider variety of settings.

How this will change the way you work

A quick trawl through a list of popular gamification technique implementations might help to inspire you to think of ways you could add a gaming element to your workplace.

- *Social networks* – sites such as LinkedIn and Facebook, where the number of friends or contacts you have are available for all to see, can drive a competitive desire in users to increase their contact numbers.

- *Health and well-being* – at several gyms, users are invited to record their best performances on a number of exercises and then challenge themselves to beat them on their next visit.

- *Recruitment* – the consultancy firm Bain & Company has run a pilot where staff are encouraged to play an online game with the hope of it pinpointing the key skills needed to become a successful consultant. The firm will then use these findings to refine their recruitment processes.

- *Customer reward* – loyalty points awarded to customers of retail stores gives customers a powerful and competitive incentive to increase their points tally and receive discounts as a result.

What you might say about this

'Let's set up a leaderboard showing who's the most punctual at submitting their expenses on time – maybe some gentle gamification techniques will solve this perennial problem.'

'If our business were a computer game, how would it be played?'

'How can we engage our customers through simple gaming techniques?'

Where you can find out more

Kevin Werbach and Dan Hunter, *For the Win: How Game Thinking Can Revolutionize Your Business*, Wharton Digital Press, 2012.

Jane McGonigal, *Reality is Broken: Why Games Make Us Better and How They Can Change the World*, Penguin Press, 2011.

IDEA #87
Working from home or shirking from home?

A randomised experiment from China suggests working from home actually works.

What you need to know

James Liang, co-founder and current chairman of the NASDAQ-listed Chinese travel agency Ctrip, wanted to find out if optional homeworking was a sensible policy to implement for his 13,000 employees. With the aid of willing researchers from his alma mater, Stanford, a randomised experiment was set up to this effect. More than 250 workers were split into the trial and control groups for the nine-month experiment; the former worked four days a week from home, the latter were located on site. Both groups used the same IT equipment, dealt with the same type and complexity of work and operated under the same pay conditions. Four fascinating results were discovered as a result of the experiment.

1. The performance of the homeworkers increased by 13 per cent over the period – this was driven by an improvement in the number of minutes worked during their shifts, resulting from fewer breaks and sick days.

2. The increase in homeworkers' performance had no negative impact on the performance of the remaining office workers.

3. The attrition rate of the homeworkers fell by 50 per cent compared to the office workers, with the homeworkers also reporting greater work satisfaction.

4. Ctrip estimated a saving of $2,000 per homeworking employee during the period, largely from reduced overheads.

In short, Ctrip's experience found that homeworking leads to greater productivity, better retention rates, improved work satisfaction and substantial cost savings. Not a bad return.

Why it matters

In the US, the proportion of workers who predominantly work from home has doubled over the past 30 years to around 4.3 per cent and the proportion of the workforce who operate from home at least a day a week is up to 10 per cent. Myriad pressures such as the desire for greater work–life balance, childcare and organisational operating costs are pointing to the need for a more evidence-based appraisal of the benefits or disadvantages of homeworking. While one must always be careful about extrapolating the results from one geographical region to another, the findings of the Stanford study's research in China provides a compelling case that working from home should be considered as a viable option for many firms.

How this will change the way you work

- *Consider homeworking.* This may not be a sensible option for all companies and in all industries, but since the range of professions regularly adopting homeworking has widened to include highly skilled work such as software engineering and consulting, and the technology needed to support this is readily available, it is easier than ever to give employees the option.

- *Give people the choice.* Another interesting result of the experiment was that, after the nine-month trial, more than half of the group working from home decided to return to the office, given the choice. Once back in the office, the performance scores of the tested group continued to improve. Seemingly there was a bounce in performance simply from giving employees the choice.

- *Run randomised trials.* James Liang found an innovative way to answer a common question, 'how do I know if this will work?', before implementing a company-wide optional homeworking policy at Ctrip. Rather than call in an army of management consultants or slow down decision-making with reams of detailed analysis and workforce modelling, Liang found some willing academics to run a rigorous, evidenced-based experiment that would offer an answer to his question. Such sound policy-making is rare in business.

What you might say about this

'As long as you deliver the work to a high standard, where you work is a moot point.'

'Maybe we've overstated the potential disadvantages of home working.'

'What should we do? Let's run an experiment to find out.'

Where you can find out more

'Does working from home work? Evidence from a Chinese experiment', Nicholas Bloom, James Liang, John Roberts and Zhichun Jenny Ying, Stanford University research paper, July 2012.

IDEA #88
The paradox of meritocracy – how doing right can lead to wrong

Companies that profess strong meritocratic values may – perversely – end up discriminating against women.

What you need to know

The social changes that have taken place in the 50-plus years since the British sociologist Michael Young satirically coined the term 'meritocracy' have led to values such as 'equality and diversity' becoming firmly embedded – in rhetoric at least – in most business environments. However, despite a plethora of legal and commercial reforms outlawing workplace discrimination on the grounds of gender, for example, there remains a substantial pay gap between men and women in most commercial sectors. The reasons for this have long been hypothesised – and are yet to be firmly concluded upon – although research by two academics from the Massachusetts Institute of Technology and Indiana University have led to a startling conclusion: organisations that pride themselves on being 'meritocratic' may in fact discriminate more against women than organisations making no such claims.

Across three experiments featuring participants with real-life managerial experience – MBA students – the researchers found a puzzling 'paradox of meritocracy'. The participants were told they were working for a fictitious large North American service sector organisation, 'ServiceOne', and given performance evaluation reports of three employees. One employee had performed poorly for the year and the other two had near-identical performance reports; of these two, one employee was male, the other female. The participants were informed that they had a bonus pot of $1,000 dollars to divide between the three employees. The participants were divided into two groups: one group was told the core corporate values of ServiceOne and received a specific briefing that the firm prized meritocratic fairness highly; the other group was also told the firm's corporate values, but in this instance no meritocratic ideals were emphasised.

In the group that had had the importance of meritocracy emphasised to them, bonuses for the comparably performing employees produced unexpected results: the male employee was paid on average $46 more in bonuses than the female employee. For the other group of participants, the female employee was paid a non-statistically significant amount of $2 more than the male employee.

Why it matters

Castilla and Bernard – the authors of the ServiceOne study – have hypothesised two reasons for this counter-intuitive behaviour. First, they describe the impact of 'moral credentials' (which Monin and Miller have previously explored), whereby 'individuals are more prone to express prejudiced attitudes when they feel that they have established their credentials as a non-prejudiced person'. Second, based on the research of Uhlmann and Cohen, they propose that when individuals feel they are being objective (in bonus or employment decisions, for instance) they are 'more likely to believe their beliefs are valid' – even if they are biased or discriminatory – and 'therefore more likely to act on them'. In other words, organisations that self-proclaim themselves as valuing meritocracy and objectivity – without clear evidence to back this up – may create conditions which lead employees into the false belief that any judgements they make must therefore also be meritocratic and objective.

How this will change the way you work

- *Beware the trap of mere rhetoric.* Saying that your organisation is an 'equal opportunities employer' or it is 'against discrimination of all kinds' are basic necessities of business these days, but to really demonstrate these principles you need to go beyond the rhetoric. In fact, the rhetoric itself could act as a dangerous mask for increasing discriminatory and biased actions.

- *Increase transparency.* Create and publish openly within your organisation the criteria that you use for employment decisions such as hiring, promotions and bonuses.

- *Focus on objective performance evaluation.* Look to minimise opportunities for human biases. The ServiceOne experiment is a case in point – giving individuals the opportunity to make judgements on bonus sizes can lead to potential biases. Had there been a clear, quantified link between performance evaluation (quantified against certain criteria) and bonus values, the scope for this bias would have been removed.

What you might say about this

'What do we actually mean when we say we're a "meritocratic organisation"?'

'Beware unintended consequences – just because we say we're being objective doesn't actually mean we are.'

'Let's try to reduce the risk of bias in our employee evaluations.'

Where you can find out more

'The paradox of meritocracy in organizations', Emilio J. Castilla and Stephen Bernard, *Administrative Science Quarterly*, Vol. 55, No. 4, 2010.

'Moral credentials and the expression of prejudice', B. Monin and D.T. Miller, *Journal of Personality and Social Psychology*, Vol. 81, No. 1, 2001.

'"I think it, therefore it's true": Effects of self-perceived objectivity on hiring discrimination', Eric Luis Uhlmann and Geoffrey L. Cohen, *Organizational Behavior and Human Decision Processes*, Vol. 104, 2007.

IDEA #89
Power, CEOs, boards and extreme strategic deviance

The best-performing companies balance CEO and board power effectively.

What you need to know

Romantic notions abound of crusading, heroic, business leaders who overcome adversity and doubters to bring their firms to greatness. Cue footage of Jack Welch of General Electric, Steve Jobs of Apple or Bill Gates of Microsoft, but is it really such a great thing to have a dominant CEO?

Analysing the results of 51 large, publicly traded computer firms in the US from 1997 to 2003, researchers from two Canadian universities wanted to test the effect of having either a weakly or strongly empowered CEO and board on firm performance. Firm performance was defined across three metrics: return on assets; return on investment; and return on sales. CEO power was calculated by five indicators: status of the CEO relative to other senior top management team (TMT) members; compensation; number of titles ascribed to the CEO; percentage of the firm's shares owned by the CEO and family; and whether the CEO was the founder or related to the founder of the firm. Board power was calculated on the basis of three variables: whether the CEO was also the chair; the proportion of outside (i.e., external to the firm) directors; and the percentage of shares held by outside directors. Using these definitions, the researchers made a number of surprising discoveries.

- Powerful CEOs are more likely than non-powerful CEOs to lead a firm towards 'strategic deviance' compared with industry peers. In other words, firms end up with marketing strategies or investment strategies that are substantially out-of-kilter with the rest of the competition. Significantly, these deviations are likely to lead to 'performance extremes' – either spectacular success or spectacular failure.

- The potentially harmful effects of powerful CEOs can be tempered by powerful boards – these are likely to rein in and reduce strategic deviance. This is not the case for weak boards, however, which are liable to be ineffective in altering a powerful CEO's ability to generate strategic deviance.

- Intriguingly, the firms with the best performance appeared to have both weak CEOs and weak boards. In instances such as these it seems likely that other executive team members contributed to good decision-making.

Why it matters

- *Balance the power.* In the post-Enron age, corporate governance matters more than ever. Understanding the interplay between board and CEO power provides a vital insight into how companies should be structured and governed. The research conducted by Tang *et al.* highlights the need for strong boards – ones not afraid to challenge CEOs and provide a counterbalance to their views. While a strong CEO may be able to map out a path to glory for an organisation, with power unchecked it might instead be a path to ruin.

How this will change the way you work

Boards should regularly undertake self-assessments of their own effectiveness. Warning signs of weak boards are likely to be ones that largely rubber stamp CEOs' proposals without discussion or debate, which have members with poor experience of the relevant industry or boards where the CEO is also the chair. Moderating CEO power should not be just a question of controlling egos – it should also be about doing what is the best for the company and its shareholders.

What you might say about this

'Have we concentrated too much power in the CEO role? How can we sensibly moderate the role's influence?'

'CEOs with dominant personalities might be great for brand reputation, but that doesn't mean they're great for a firm's long-term strategy.'

'We rarely hear about CEO or board dilemmas from this company, but they've performed very well historically. They probably have a very consensual and effective approach to decision-making at the executive team level.'

Where you can find out more

'Dominant CEO, deviant strategy, and extreme performance: The moderating role of a powerful board', Jianyun Tang, Mary Crossan and W. Glenn Rowe, *Journal of Management Studies*, Vol. 48, No. 7, 2011.

IDEA #90
The myth of CEO experience

Firms that hire CEOs with prior experience as chief executives tend to underperform financially.

What you need to know

In the short term, markets react much more favourably to CEO appointments where the new chief is external and has prior CEO experience than if the appointment is an internal candidate with no prior top experience. However, research by Monika Hamori and Burak Koyuncu suggests that in the longer term, the benefits quickly evaporate. Tracking S&P500 companies' return on assets performance for three years after CEO appointment, the researchers found companies that appointed CEOs with prior CEO experience delivered a median annual average return on assets of 3.9 per cent, compared with a 5.4 per cent return for companies with CEOs with no prior CEO experience. This was even after adjusting for overall industry performance.

Why it matters

The insider–outsider debate is a perennial one in companies considering their next CEO. While internal appointments may have the 'knowledge and feel of the company', they are unlikely to have prior experience of the very top job. External appointments, conversely, are believed to help bring in 'new ways of thinking'. Hamori and Koyuncu suggest their research demonstrates that prior CEO experience may 'lead to the formation of knowledge corridors and decision-making templates that make it difficult for individuals to take in inconsistent information or take actions that are different from past ones in a changed context. This, in turn, undermines performance.' In other words, picking a seasoned CEO as the top boss may have a negative effect on corporate performance.

How this will change the way you work

- New CEOs with prior top experience will need to work especially hard to unlearn many of the traits and habits of their old firms. What worked well in one firm may not be replicable in another. Hamori and Koyuncu found that the negative effects of prior CEO experience were actually exacerbated when the CEO came from a similar-sized company (resulting in median return on assets of 2.9 per cent). Hiring a top chief because of experience in a 'similar, but different' firm may actually be the worst of both worlds.

- Succession planning may be the best way forward and it should start early. Organisations should look to identify 'high potential individuals' early in their careers and develop them accordingly. Not only may internal appointments give the best outcomes but also the recruitment process for internal hires is invariably cheaper than for external ones.

- If you do want to appoint a CEO with prior CEO experience, consider first introducing him or her to the organisation in a COO or deputy CEO role for at least six months. This way not only can the person pick up the feel and culture of the organisation, the time can serve as an extended assessment of whether he or she really is the right person for the top job.

What you might say about this

'The right appointment could be right under our noses.'

'External isn't always best.'

'Let's not chase short-term gain at the expense of long-term stability and success.'

Where you can find out more

'Experience matters? The impact of prior CEO experience on firm performance', M. Hamori and B. Koyuncu, *Academy of Management Annual Meeting*, 2010.

'Does experience matter? CEO successions by former CEOs', Eahab Elsaid, Xiaoxin Wang and Wallace N. Davidson III, *Managerial Finance*, Vol. 37, No. 10, 2011.

IDEA #91
Change, language and history

How rhetoric can help embed institutional change.

What you need to know

In the 2011 *Administrative Science Quarterly's* award-winning paper for scholarly contribution, Roy Suddaby and Royston Greenwood analysed the discourse following the 1997 high-profile acquisition of a Canadian law firm by a large accounting firm, Ernst & Young. In doing so, they helped to define some key rhetorical techniques that can be used when arguing for or against institutional change.

The Ernst & Young acquisition was highly controversial at the time as it struck at the heart of questions about what form new multidisciplinary organisations should take. Hitherto, accounting and legal firms operated as separate entities, yet Ernst & Young's move broke new ground by proposing the creation of a multidisciplinary professional service firm. The proposition was hotly contested and a commission was set up by the American Bar Association and the US Securities and Exchange Commission to understand what the appropriate operating practices of these new multidisciplinary firms should be. Opponents and proponents of the merger took to the stand to voice their opinions on the matter. Through analysing the transcripts of the Commission, Suddaby and Greenwood devised a framework to help understand different rhetorical strategies for 'theorisations of change' – in other words, how people talk about and seek to legitimise change. These were:

- *ontological* – based on 'fundamental beliefs' about the way the world should be; usually a conservative force, against change;

- *historical* – refers to 'tradition' and invokes the names of great characters from the past; usually used to moderate radical change and instead suggest 'evolutionary or path-dependent change';

- *teleological* – appealing to a 'final cause' or vision of a path towards a given goal, but teleological language is often couched in arguments that encourage a dramatic break from the past, aimed at facilitating transformational change;

- *cosmological* – highlighting the inevitability of certain forces, such as globalisation, which lead to a clear and necessary course of action;

- *value-based* – which can be invoked by either side in an argument, and usually involve claiming that 'our values are better than their values'.

Why it matters

A 2012 paper, led by Tim Morris of the Saïd Business School, also looked into the details of how 'professional service firms [move from] traditional partnerships to professionally managed businesses' – another example of profound institutional change. This research concluded that powerful decision-makers are key in ushering in change and in terms of the rhetoric they use, 'change must be firmly grounded in the cultural traditions and values of the firm'. In other words, and to use Suddaby and Greenwood's model, successful change involves appealing to 'historical' and 'value-based' theorisations of change when explaining why the status quo is no longer an option.

How this will change the way you work

- *Consider the levers of change.* Reflect back on a major institutional change (such as a takeover or transformational strategy) you have either been a part of or witnessed from afar. How did the different parties on either side of the argument use language to describe what was taking place? Suddaby and Greenwood's analysis provides a helpful framework to think about how to describe change across a series of theorisations.

- *Appeal to organisational history and values.* If you're trying to build momentum for change and articulate why change is necessary, it would appear that speaking to the history and values of an organisation would be a good place to start.

What you might say about this

'While we are changing, this change is very much in tune with our values and what we stand for, and have always stood for, as an organisation.'

'He's only really using ontological arguments for legitimising change. I don't think that will suffice to win over the sceptics. He needs a broader suite of theorisations of change to really address the concerns of all the doubters.'

'Change always looks to the future, but maybe we should think about couching change in terms of our successful past.'

Where you can find out more

'Rhetorical strategies of legitimacy', Roy Suddaby and Royston Greenwood, *Administrative Science Quarterly*, March 2005.

'Episodic and systemic power in the transformation of professional service firms', Thomas B. Lawrence, Namrata Malhotra and Tim Morris, *Journal of Management Studies*, Vol. 49, No. 1, 2012.

IDEA #92
MBA students and the cheating bug

How and why MBA students cheat.

What you need to know

In the 2006 *Academy of Management Learning and Education* Paper of the Year, Donald McCabe, Kenneth Butterfield and Linda Treviño brought new insight to the long-held perception that Master of Business Administration (MBA) students are cheaters. Using a definition of cheating that included 13 criteria (5 related to cheating on tests and exams – such as copying a peer's work or using crib notes and eight related to written coursework – such as plagiarism or falsifying bibliographies) the researchers invited students to fill in an anonymous survey across '54 colleges and universities in the United States and Canada ... of which 32 had graduate business programs'.

The responses back totalled 5,300, of which 623 were students of graduate business programmes. An astonishing 56 per cent of business students confessed to cheating at least once in the previous year, compared to 47 per cent of non-business students. By comparison, in other disciplines 54 per cent of graduate engineering students admitted to cheating, whereas a much lower 39 per cent of humanities and social sciences revealed they were cheats.

Why it matters

Ethical business is good business. The need for instilling good virtues and principles in young people in schools is universally accepted, yet for some reason most of the time people turn a blind eye to cheating in graduate business programmes – unless, of course, they are found out. This research suggests there is a real problem with cheating in business schools in the US and Canada that needs to be flushed out.

How this will change the way you work

- *Break the peer behavioural cycle.* When probing the causes of cheating, the researchers found the overwhelming driver to be perceived peer behaviour. In effect, graduate business students felt it was acceptable to cheat because they believed other students were cheating, too. This suggests there may be a cultural problem in some business schools. Administrators and deans should tackle the issue head on, forcing students to recognise the scale of the issue and the consequences of being caught. Employers should also be wary. Everyone has the potential to cheat and having an MBA doesn't reduce this risk.

What you might say about this

'Cheating in an exam points to a moral failure in an individual – can we run the risk of having someone who does this in our organisation?'

'Would you falsify a financial report? How can I be sure that you wouldn't if you think it's OK to falsify a source or citation?'

'Peer behaviour drives bad behaviour. We need to role model what good looks like.'

Where you can find out more

'Academic dishonesty in graduate business programs: Prevalence, causes, and proposed action', Donald L. McCabe, Kenneth D. Butterfield and Linda Klebe Treviño, *Academy of Management Learning and Education*, Vol. 5, No. 3, 2006.

IDEA #93
Is your office making you sick?

Sick building syndrome can lead to absenteeism.

What you need to know

Sick building syndrome (SBS) – the idea that buildings can make us feel unwell – developed as a concept through a combination of worker activism and workplace and epidemiology studies in the 1980s, to the extent that SBS was one of the most investigated occupational health issues in the United States by the 1990s. In 1984, the World Health Organization released a report on SBS, which suggested that up to 30 per cent of all remodelled buildings globally could be the cause. Through a fascinating and quirky historical look at the development of the campaigns around SBS, Michelle Murphy of the University of Toronto has demonstrated how forces of feminism, ventilation engineering, worker protests and occupational science raised SBS to the top of the corporate agenda in the 1990s. With a large number of women reported to be sufferers of SBS, symptoms are known to include headaches, rashes, poor concentration, eye and throat infections and fatigue. One of the key characteristics of SBS is that symptoms usually improve on leaving the buildings in question.

Why it matters

No single causal factor has been directly attributed to SBS, but numerous studies have largely concluded that a combination of issues is to blame. On the whole, this is most apparent in relatively new office buildings with poor ventilation (i.e., windows do not open) and air conditioning. Specifically, this means there might be a lack of natural air; low humidity; temperature fluctuations; dirty carpets; electrostatic charges; poor lighting; airborne chemicals (such as from cleaning materials); and flickering visual display units on screens. While women report more symptoms of SBS, this may be as a result of greater numbers of females working in SBS-prone office environments as opposed to any specific gender-related resistance differences.

How this will change the way you work

Surprisingly, the vast majority of offices that have high levels of reported SBS comply with design standards for ventilation, temperature and lighting. So to tackle SBS you need to be especially vigilant. A number of actions can help here.

- *Check the cleanliness of the building* – including air filters, vacuum cleaners and whether cleaning materials are carefully stored away in an appropriate place.

- *Check the operations of the office* – make sure that all air conditioning and ventilation systems are working effectively.

- *Check your employees* – run a survey to understand the scale of the problem (if any). *The Lancet* recommends asking a) 'In the past 12 months have you had more than two episodes of … [give a list of the symptoms mentioned above]'; and 'If 'yes' to a), was it better on days away from the office?'

What you might say about this

'We seem to be doing everything right about workplace cleanliness, but benchmarked against our peers our sick day rates seem to be high. Do we have a sick building syndrome problem?'

'We should encourage everyone to go outside for some fresh air when they take breaks – let's build a suitable outdoor area to make this a pleasant experience.'

'Open some windows!'

Where you can find out more

Michelle Murphy, *Sick Building Syndrome and the Problem of Uncertainty: Environmental, Technoscience, and Women Workers*, Duke University Press, 2006.

'Sick building syndrome', P.S. Burge, *Occupational and Environmental Medicine*, Vol. 61, No. 2, 2004.

'Sick-building syndrome', Carrie A. Redlich, Judy Sparer and Mark R. Cullen, *The Lancet*, Vol. 349, No. 9057, 1997.

IDEA #94
Strong culture, reliable performance

The strength of a firm's corporate culture can help it to deliver reliable financial and operational performance in times of stability, but can hinder it under volatile conditions.

What you need to know

What is the impact of having a 'strong culture' (commonly defined as 'a set of norms and values that are widely shared and strongly held throughout the organisation') in a firm? In order to find out, Jesper Sørensen analysed the performance of 'large, publicly traded firms in 18 markets', across a range of metrics from return on investment, to operating cash flow, to debt-to-asset ratios. Sørensen then combined these performance metrics with an evaluation of companies' cultural strength. Cultural strength was, in part, determined by C-suite officers' responses to a survey on three indicators of corporate culture that asked if:

1. managers in a firm commonly speak of their company's style or way of doing things;
2. the firm has made its values known through a creed or credo and had made a serious attempt to get managers to follow them;
3. the firm has been managed according to long-standing policies and practices other than those just of the current CEO.

Sørensen found that strong corporate cultures – under stable macro-economic conditions – led to reliable (defined as low variation) corporate performance. However, under volatile market conditions, strong corporate cultures may in fact hold back performance.

Why it matters

The merits of strong corporate cultures have been commonly identified in non-quantitative terms. By contrast, Sørensen's research clearly identified the correlation between quantifiable performance metrics and corporate culture. This has an important repercussion in practical terms. Sørensen's analysis resulted in the observation that the strong-culture firms have more stable cash flows – the implications of which mean that 'they are less likely to underinvest' in new products or research. However there is a flip-side to this; strong cultures – because they often engender set ways of working – can potentially inhibit creativity and a willingness to take risks. Under stable operating environments this may not be an issue, but when markets turn, the inability to be flexible and responsive can prevent companies from innovating their way out of problems.

How this will change the way you work

- *Identify the strength of your existing corporate culture.* Start by answering the questions asked of the C-suite officers in Sørensen's survey. How does your firm compare? If you note a strong corporate culture, do you think this could inhibit corporate creativity? If you feel it does, encourage senior officers to reconsider the company's values – could you be doing more to allow innovation to flourish?

What you might say about this

'Strong corporate culture isn't just a nice buzzword – it can really improve bottom-line performance.'

'How do we ensure we keep our values strong without stifling creativity?'

'How would you rate the strength of our company's culture?'

Where you can find out more

'The strength of corporate culture and the reliability of firm performance', Jesper B. Sørensen, *Administrative Science Quarterly*, Vol. 47, No. 1, 2002.

IDEA #95
Strategy, leaders and leadership harmony

Successful strategic change requires organisation leaders to be fully on board.

What you need to know

How do you successfully implement major strategic change? That was the question a team of researchers led by Charles O'Reilly of the Stanford Graduate School of Business sought to answer by analysing strategy implementation at Kaiser Permanente (KP), a large healthcare organisation. With more than a million members and nearly 20 clinics, KP was facing increased competition from rival providers. Following corporate discussions, KP decided on a new strategy: rather than focusing on being a low-cost healthcare provider, KP sought to differentiate itself through excellent quality and service. In practice this meant significant operational changes such as new scheduling systems and call centres. Success was to be measured in terms of patient satisfaction.

Why it matters

Tomes of research have been dedicated to what leadership is, but, until now, relatively few studies have focused on rigorously analysing how different leadership styles impact operational performance. In politically complex fields such as healthcare organisations – where managers are often assumed to be at odds with clinicians – how leaders act is a crucial question. The KP study resulted in three insightful discoveries.

1. Notions of organisational leadership need to be more carefully broken down. There are several forms of 'leadership' operating in different parts of an organisation. Crudely these can be split into three tiers: corporate level (e.g., C-suite); business unit level (e.g., director of finance); and departmental level (e.g., head of finance and informatics). How these different tiers interact with each other is of vital importance to how successfully change happens.

2. The more competent a CEO and departmental head are perceived to be by the organisation, the more likely it is that key frontline staff (in the KP case, these were physicians) will support the implementation strategy.

3. Set organisational objectives (in this instance, improving patient satisfaction) are more likely to be achieved if the rest of the organisation believes there is strong harmony across the leadership tiers. In essence, for employees to help meet organisational objectives they need to believe that their leaders are united in a common endeavour.

How this will change the way you work

- *Seek consensus.* The findings from the Kaiser Permanente study highlight the importance of perceived leadership harmony in organisations. Before a new strategy can begin implementation, a chief executive should be convinced that all the organisation leaders are fully behind it. If they are not, employees will become disillusioned as they receive mixed messages from the organisation's upper echelons and, as a result, do not accept the need for change. As a consequence, performance is likely to be below par.

What you might say about this

'We need to make sure every manager in the company fully understands why we're doing what we're doing.'

'I need you to be behind this strategy, otherwise it won't work.'

'Harmony is the key.'

Where you can find out more

'How leadership matters: The effects of leaders' alignment on strategy implementation', Charles A. O'Reilly, David F. Caldwell, Jennifer A. Chatman, Margaret Lapiz and William Self, *The Leadership Quarterly*, Vol. 21, No. 1, 2010.

IDEA #96
Need to manage a negative rumour? Challenge its credibility

How rumours turn fiction into fact.

What you need to know

Academic research on how rumours originate generally agrees on the theory that they arise in order to fill a void created by the absence of information in uncertain situations. Three researchers from the Kellogg School of Management and Stanford University have gone a step further and investigated the root causes that make rumours turn from mere fiction into perceived fact. Through four separate experiments, Derek Rucker and David Dubois concluded that although individuals 'transmit their core beliefs when they communicate with each other, they often fail to transmit their certainty or uncertainty about those beliefs'.

In other words, imagine a chain of three consumers spreading a rumour that a bakery has been serving stale products to customers.

Consumer 1 might tell Consumer 2, 'I heard that Mrs Bread's has been selling gone-off cakes and several people got food poisoning as a result [core belief], but I'm not sure how much I believe my source [certainty or uncertainty].' However, by the time Consumer 2 passes the same message on to Consumer 3, he or she is likely to have kept the core belief but lost the certainty or uncertainty element of the rumour. Thus he or she might state, 'I heard Mrs Bread's has been selling gone-off products that make people ill.' Nowhere does he or she mention Consumer 1's concerns about the provenance or credibility of the claim. Thus this failure to pass on 'certainty or uncertainty' in rumours is deemed to be critical in how fiction turns into fact.

Why it matters

Famously, in October 2008, a rumour spread that the late Steve Jobs would have to step down from Apple due to ill health, which led the company to temporarily lose $9 billion from its stock market value. Anyone in PR or brand management knows only too well the huge impact perceptions – grounded in reality or not – can have on the value of a brand. Traditional PR turnaround strategies following an attack on a brand focus on what to do once disaster has struck: act fast; localise the impact; launch a counter-strategy. This research suggests ways in which companies can act even sooner by nipping threatening rumours in the bud through challenging their certainty.

How this will change the way you work

- Question the premise of any rumour. Brands should directly engage with consumers and challenge them on the credibility, authenticity and provenance of potentially harmful and negative claims. Raising the issue of the certainty of a rumour will help to discredit it.

- Further research suggests that it is possible to successfully prompt consumers to focus on the certainty of their beliefs; doing this will help to balance out the seemingly inherent preference to transmit ideas rather than question them. With social media allowing companies to communicate with consumers with greater ease than ever before, a platform exists from which to put this advice into practice.

- On a more day-to-day basis, the next time you hear something surprising in the workplace, ask your colleague what the source is and if he or she genuinely believes the rumour.

What you might say about this

'Send out a press release denying the rumour and questioning the reliability of the source.'

'I don't believe that.'

'On a scale of one to ten how certain are you that this is true?'

Where you can find out more

'From rumors to facts, and facts to rumors: The role of certainty decay in consumer communications', David Dubois, Derek D. Rucker and Zakary L. Tormala, *Journal of Marketing Research*, Vol. 48, No. 6, 2011.

IDEA #97
How management myths are formed

The Hawthorne Effect – one of the most frequently cited management studies – is not all it seems.

What you need to know

Between 1924 and 1932, Elton Mayo and Fritz J. Roethlisberger – both professors at Harvard Business School – undertook a series of groundbreaking workplace studies at General Electric's enormous Hawthorne Works factory just outside of Chicago. Of the large number of experiments that took place, one of the most famous was based on illumination. Women workers (some became minor celebrities as a result of the studies) were asked to form teams, with their output measured by completed relays deposited down a chute. The impact of a number of variables on output levels was then tested. These included giving the workers five-minute breaks, providing break-time snacks and dimming or increasing light in the plant room. The key finding was that whatever the variable tested, productivity usually increased for a short time afterwards. Mayo hypothesised that the combination of attention being focused on the workers from the experiments and the team camaraderie which developed from the teams being put together led to the productivity increases.

Why it matters

Since Mayo's study, the 'Hawthorne Effect' has been used and abused as a term in all manner of management fields. Taken as gospel, everything from the mantras 'you need to treat workers well' to 'if you just focus on a problem things will get better' have been linked back to the so-called 'findings' of the Hawthorne studies. However, the experiments were never formally written up (the original data were assumed lost) and were only based on the output of five workers – two of whom were replaced during the experiment for poor behaviour.

However, Steven D. Levitt and John A. List managed to recover the data from the experiments and, after re-running the analyses, found there was no 'Hawthorne effect' that could not be accounted for by other factors – such as what day of the week output was measured from. In their words, 'we find little support for the Hawthorne effect when the data are properly interpreted. We find, however, that a naïve misreading of the data might lead someone to falsely conclude that a Hawthorne effect is present.'

How this will change the way you work

- *One myth doesn't mean it's all fiction.* This does not necessarily mean the principle of the 'Hawthorne effect' – that people change their behaviour as a result of attention from others – is utterly fictitious. Other research has demonstrated that those experimented on may change their behaviour as a result of being under observation (Martin Orne, a professor and practitioner of psychiatry and psychology, has undertaken studies highlighting this effect – known as the 'demand effect') and so researchers should always control for this in any experiment. However, the point is the 'Hawthorne effect' – at least in the sense that it was based on the Hawthorne studies – does not exist. It is a management myth. So, the next time you hear somebody invoke its name, you may wish to call them on this.

What you might say about this

'What exactly do you mean when you say the "Hawthorne Effect"?'

'We need to be wary of the "demand effect" – if we're trying to do something different, people could react in unexpected ways.'

'What other management myths do we take as gospel?'

Where you can find out more

Elton Mayo, *The Human Problems of an Industrial Civilization*, Macmillan, 1946.

'Was there a Hawthorne effect?', Stephen R.G. Jones, *American Journal of Sociology*, Vol. 98, No. 3, 1992.

'Was there really a Hawthorne effect at the Hawthorne plant? An analysis of the original illumination experiments', Steven D. Levitt and John A. List, *American Economic Journal: Applied Economics*, Vol. 3, No. 1, 2011.

IDEA #98
Why you should offer surgery with a free lollipop

When it's hard to evaluate different services, consumers focus on unique features.

What you need to know

How do consumers choose between different service providers? According to researchers from the University of International Business and Economics, University of Queensland and Kellogg School of Management, the role of 'uncertainty' in evaluation is critical. Some services can be evaluated during actual experience – buying a product such as a car, for instance. These services have low degrees of 'uncertainty' compared to surgical services, for example, where it is not (feasibly) possible to trial the service beforehand.

Differing from 'low-uncertainty' services, for 'high-uncertainty' services (and usually higher-risk, as well) consumers base their provider evaluations primarily on the reputation of a company and, second, on the unique features they offer with their services. The finding that when consumers struggle to evaluate different service providers they rely on faith in a corporate brand is probably not surprising, but the second mode of evaluation – unique features – is much more revealing.

Why it matters

The Harvard academic Michael Porter has popularised three basic strategies that businesses can employ to gain competitive advantage in the marketplace: cost leadership (i.e., having the lowest costs); differentiation (i.e., offering a unique service); and focus (i.e., dominating a niche marketplace). The findings from this study offer a new insight into Porter's model: for 'high-uncertainty' services (i.e., those that are difficult to evaluate, less tangible or procured less frequently by consumers), differentiation may be the key strategy to employ. Rather than being cost-conscious for these sorts of services, consumers may respond more positively to unique features offered that help to differentiate service providers from their competitors.

How this will change the way you work

The authors of the research suggest their findings have implications for both high- and low-uncertainty service providers:

- Low-uncertainty service providers 'such as retail banks should focus on improving features that can easily be compared with their competitors. For example, staying open longer or offering more competitive interest rates.'

- High-uncertainty service providers 'such as those provided by insurance companies' should focus on strategies that 'create innovative and distinctive features such as personalised consulting services'.

What you might say about this

'What unique features do we offer as part of our service that no one else does?'

'Are our unique selling points something that our consumers really value?'

'We need to make it easier for potential customers to be able to compare our products to our rivals so they can realise how we offer the best products around.'

Where you can find out more

'The effect of attribute alignability on service evaluation: The moderating role of uncertainty', Jin Sun, Heah Tat Keh and Angela Y. Lee, *Journal of Consumer Research*, Vol. 39, No. 4, 2012.

IDEA #99
It's why, not what, that matters

Why you do something matters much more than what you do.

What you need to know

Proving the benefit of corporate mission statements, values, identity, etc. is a tricky business. Broadly speaking, researchers on this topic are split between those who see no value whatsoever in such pronouncements and those who suggest more effort is needed to properly define 'corporate values' before testing their impact further. Eschewing hard quantitative analysis, Simon Sinek – a lecturer at Columbia University – has instead proposed a simple, intuitive and compelling framework for how great leaders and companies can inspire others called the 'Golden Circle'. According to this theory, great inspiration comes from communicating with others as follows:

> *Explaining WHY you do something > Detailing HOW you do it > Describing WHAT you do*

Tying his theory to biological research on how the brain works, Sinek suggests that the WHY and HOW elements appeal to emotions such as trust and are processed by the limbic part of the brain, while the WHAT part is processed by the part of the brain that deals with reason and rationality – the neocortex.

Why it matters

According to Sinek, most companies are dull and uninspiring in their message to customers and most only deal with the rational, 'WHAT' part of the Golden Circle. Thus, a boring company CEO might announce to investors, 'Our latest product has fantastic functionality that far outperforms its competitors.' By contrast, inspirational leaders and aspirational companies start with 'WHY'. As stated in his TEDx talk on the subject, for Sinek, Apple's message to its customers is this:

- WHY: In everything we do, we believe in challenging the status quo. We believe in thinking differently.

- HOW: The way we challenge the status quo is by making our products beautifully designed, simple to use and user-friendly.

- WHAT: We just happen to make great computers. Want to buy one?

How this will change the way you work

- To inspire, you need to move beyond the mundane. You need to start by articulating why you do something; what you believe in; what cause you are fighting for. Customers will buy into a cause and an idea, not a product. Dull leaders know what they do: 'I am the CEO of company X.' Smart leaders might know what they do and how they do it: 'I am the CEO of company X and we add value to our shareholders through offering unparalleled customer service in our field.'

- Truly inspirational leaders turn the typical communication mode on its head and, instead, start with what they and their company believe in; the services and products offered flow from this, not the other way around.

- Apply Sinek's Golden Circle theory to your work life. Why do you do what you do? Why does your company do what it does? How do you communicate the purpose of the work life you lead to others? You might want to rethink this and start with why, not what.

What you might say about this

'"I have a dream" sounds more inspirational than "I have a plan".'

'I know what he's saying makes perfect sense, but I just don't feel excited about it. My neocortex is engaged, but limbic system is bored stiff.'

'Lots of people offer similar products to us (our "what") so we need to differentiate ourselves by "why" we do what we do.'

Where you can find out more

Simon Sinek, *Start With Why: How Great Leaders Inspire Everyone to Take Action*, Penguin Books, 2011.

'Three Fs for the mission statement: What's next?', Azaddin Salem Khalifa, *Journal of Strategy Management*, Vol. 4, No. 1, 2011.

IDEA #100
Competition in the workplace

A competitive workplace may not necessarily be a better one.

What you need to know

In the early 1970s, in a bid to increase performance, Bruce Henderson, founder of the Boston Consulting Group divided his consultants into three teams: Blue, Red and Green. For a while the competitiveness seemed to spur innovation and business success, but in the end the negative consequences far outweighed the benefits. So competitive was the environment Henderson created that the leader of the Blue team – Bill Bain – quit, taking most of his team with him to start up a completely rival firm, Bain & Company. In pursuit of a short-term injection of competition, Henderson ended up creating a rival firm that for some years put BCG in its shadow. Competition, in other words, is a dangerous motivational tool to instil in the workplace.

Why it matters

The research on competition in the workplace is certainly mixed, despite many assumptions that it is a necessary prerequisite for top performance. Pitching investment teams against each other or giving individualised bonuses might seem like a good idea, but in practice, competition can have quite destabilising effects. One study of 280 undergraduate students tested the impact of competition on creativity and found that while some competitive measures did lead to better results, others made no difference whatsoever. Preliminary research by Iwan Barankay at the Wharton School suggests that in many instances, competitive measures (such as giving frequent feedback to employees or ranking them by performance) actually *decrease* productivity.

How this will change the way you work

As a manager, if you are looking to inject a bit of competition, either between teams, individuals or against rival firms, there are three important things to bear in mind:

1. *Be fair.* Nothing will upset staff more than unfair performance measures. For instance, if you were measuring drinks sales between bartenders, you shouldn't only use raw sales figures to infer performance. Instead you should adjust for time of day (because one would sell more in the evening than in the early afternoon) day of the week and season, for example.

2. *Make things quantifiable and objective.* Your measurements need to be clearly explained and carefully shared. Performance managing on the basis of subjective evaluations is a recipe for disaster – make sure people record scores against common criteria.

3. *Watch out for unintended consequences.* Many of these will be painfully predictable, but so obvious that they are often not properly managed. It doesn't take a genius to hypothesise that financially incentivising insurance package sellers might lead to some actions that do not always put the customers' best interests at heart (see for instance the payment protection insurance mis-selling scandal in the UK). Set up internal review systems that pre-empt and prevent such corrosive behaviour.

What you might say about this

'What are the risks of implementing a more aggressive performance management system?'

'Who do we want people to compete against: themselves, their peers or our industry competitors?'

'Competition can create a winner–loser mentality within teams. Is that really what we want?'

Where you can find out more

'Win or lose the battle for creativity: The power and perils of intergroup competition', Markus Baer, Roger Th. A. J. Leenders, Greg R. Oldham and Abhijeet K. Vadera, *Academy of Management Journal*, Vol. 53, No. 4, 2010.

Walter Kiechel III, *The Lords of Strategy: The Secret Intellectual History of the New Corporate World*, Harvard Business School Press, 2010.

IDEA #101
Face-time counts

Presenteeism – even if you're not actually interacting with anyone – still has a positive impact on bosses.

What you need to know

With increasingly long commutes, a desire to create healthier work–life balances, and a drive towards flexible schedules for working parents, over the past 20 years companies have been going out of their way to say that 'it's not the hours you put in that count', but the 'output you deliver'. However, research conducted in *Human Relations*' 2010 Paper of the Year suggests that, subconsciously, managers and colleagues still make 'trait inferences' (in other words, draw conclusions about individuals) based on the amount of face-time they put in at the office. As you can guess, it's those people who stay the latest and work the longest who get the most positive conclusions drawn about them – even if they're not doing anything of any real value.

Why it matters

Authors of the study distinguish between two types of passive face-time (labelled 'passive' because you are not interacting with anyone at this time):

- *expected face-time* – simply being at work during standard business hours;
- *extracurricular face-time* – being at work outside of expected hours, such as late nights, early mornings or weekends.

The study asked managers across dozens of industries to evaluate employees based on descriptions of them that often contained information about the expected or extracurricular face-time activities of these employees. The results were clear: individuals who put in 'expected face-time' were 9 per cent more likely to be evaluated as being 'dependable' or 'responsible' by managers than those who did not; and employees who put in 'extracurricular face-time' were 25 per cent more likely to be attributed the traits of being 'committed' or 'dedicated'.

During the study, no given employee descriptions contained explicit information regarding an individual's 'dependability' or 'commitment' and so it can be assumed that these traits were inferred by the managers based on the information they were given about an employee's expected or extracurricular face-time. Thus one can conclude that managers – possibly subconsciously – give employees brownie points for showing up and even more for staying late. This is despite the fact that there is no evidence passive face-time actually leads to better performance.

How this will change the way you work

- Managers and co-workers should make a mental note of the dangers of 'subconscious spontaneous trait inference'. Your natural default is to assume that someone who stays late is a hard worker, but this may not be the case and you should be aware of this potential bias.

- Organisations should ensure that employee evaluations rely on more than just qualitative descriptions of behaviour or traits, as these are prone to bias. Instead, as far as possible, evaluations should be objective, quantitatively based and focused on employee outputs, not inputs.

- Despite all this, employees might still wish to take note of the sneakier implications of the research. Regardless of the rhetoric, it is inevitable that some biases will occur when evaluating an individuals' performance and these may arise from the amount of 'face-time' you put in. You might wish to be clever about this: when the boss is about, put in the face-time. When they're away, head home early!

What you might say about this

'All employee evaluations need to be output-based. At the start of each year we need to set objectives and targets for each person, based on performance, not input hours.'

'My manager is away this week. This is probably the best time to work from home.'

'I don't care about "face-time" assessment biases – I think people should be in the office at all expected times.'

Where you can find out more

'How passive "face time" affects perceptions of employees: Evidence of spontaneous trait inference', D. Kimberly, D.M. Elsbach, J. Cable and W. Sherman, *Human Relations*, Vol. 63, No. 6, 2010.